THE POWER

OF

HUMAN WORTH

Unleash Your Potential

JAMES M. EVANS

Eagle Quest Group, Inc.
Tampa, Florida

JAMES M. EVANS

The Power of Human Worth:
Unleash Your Potential

An Eagle Quest Group Book
Published by
Eagle Quest Group, Inc.
December 2011

EAGLE QUEST
G R O U P, I N C.

Eagle Quest Group, Inc.
Email: info@eaglequestgroup.com
Web: www.eaglequestgroup.com,
on Facebook, and
on twitter.com/#!/TampaEQG

Book Cover Design by Talmadge Evans
Book Layout by Drew's Graphics

I dedicate this book to all those who are fighting to overcome the obstacles in their lives, who have been told what they can and cannot do, who are struggling to find their true calling and what gives their lives purpose and meaning. You can fulfill your dreams, you can make a difference in your life...Yes, you can! Yes, you can!

In memory of my beloved mother, Maxine Evans, who passed away on November 5, 2011.

CONTENTS

ACKNOWLEDGMENTS

First and foremost, I would like to give thanks to my Creator for giving me the strength, courage and faith to write this book.

I would like to thank all the people who, over the years, were willing to mentor me along my life's journey and guide me to become a better person and succeed in my mission to change the lives of others. Many of them supported my efforts to give hope to others by committing their time, donations and dedication and showed me that having a supportive network of good people is essential to serving others. My thanks go out to all the generous-hearted people who have influenced my thinking and career choices with their kind support and caring dedication. I owe them a great deal of gratitude for sharing with me their wisdom and knowledge.

To all my coaches, especially my middle and high school "mentor-coaches," George Walker and Joe Collins, and my college coach, Otis Washington, at Southern University, for their guidance and teaching me how to become disciplined and focused so that I was then able to overcome the daily challenges of my life. To the National Football League, my former teammates, and NFL coaches, Frank Gansz and Billie Matthews, for pushing me beyond my self-imposed limitations and showing me that I could achieve whatever I put my mind to.

To the Samuel and Yvonne Hughes family of Baton Rouge, Louisiana and the Chuck and Nancy Winship family, former owners of Beef O'Brady's restaurants, who mentored me and were such admirable role models that I will forever be grateful for their love and support at a time when I needed it the most. They made me feel like part of their families, loving me and sacrificing their time and money over many years to invest in my endeavors.

I will always cherish the friendships of Bob Conigliaro of McDonald's Casper Co.; Tallie Gainier, III; the Pete and Vernell Durand family; and Clestine Herbert. Their wisdom, ideas and suggestions have and will continue to inspire and bring out the best in me.

To Pastor Levy Webb in Baltimore, Maryland, for his wisdom and letting me bounce my spiritual ideas off him.

To my close friend Andrew Burgess of Drew's Graphics/Arts & Crafts and his family. I am indebted to him for his many sacrifices over the past 20 years. Caring and patient, he stayed up late many nights helping me on my projects. Even when his children were being born, he was there for me. He takes pride in his work with meticulous detail and outstanding graphic design.

To Betty Luddington for her Thomaston research and Iris B. Holton (The Florida Sentinel-Bulletin) for her news coverage of me and the Tampa Bay Academy of Hope (TBAH) over the years.

I thank the past and present Board of Directors who have served the TBAH so well.

A heart-felt thanks to those who devoted their time and efforts to review the manuscript prior to publication: Pat Harney, Scott Holland, Angela Jordan, Margaret Norquist, John and Misty O'Brien, Chikita Shell, Barbara Rosenke-Sweeney, Vernetta Williams, and Angela Sheble-Wilson. Their recommendations and suggestions are greatly appreciated.

With special thanks to my large family in Alabama for their continued love and to my niece Chikita Shell and nephew Talmadge Evans for all their love and talent in helping me to produce this book to help others.

To my wife, Gail, the love of my life, and my children, Triniti and Destini, who have kept me grounded and have been my support and inspiration for all my accomplishments.

I know that without the prayers and faith of those who have gone on before me I could never have been the person that I am today. These faithful men and women laid a foundation upon which my life is built. They sowed the seeds and offered me the opportunity to reap the harvest.

A Special Tribute to Coach Laura Biasci

There is a saying, "When the student is ready, the teacher will appear." I owe a great deal of gratitude and thanks to Coach Laura Biasci for agreeing to be my coach and mentor. When I began writing this book, I did not have a clear plan. Coach Laura pointed me in the right direction. She apparently saw something in me to make the personal sacrifice of her time, talent and resources to help me share my passion about Human Worth to the world. Seeing the potential in me, she juggled her schedules to help me write this book when everyone else seemed too busy to help.

What was only supposed to be a few weeks of "review" became a month and then another and another—eventually, she sacrificed two years of her time helping me write this book. With discipline and toughness, she slowly began to cultivate my writing abilities and held me accountable to organize my thoughts and beliefs about the messages I wanted to communicate to the public. Sitting with me for many months on end, guiding me, questioning my beliefs and every little word that could be unclear, she forced me to think through my premises, and as a result, she endured countless revisions, reviews and late work nights.

When I didn't follow through with anything, she pushed me hard and reminded me of my former football coaches who forced me to be disciplined and focused. I call this the "Laura Biasci directive." Coach Laura believed in me and helped me to write with clear definition and purpose; she motivated me to stay on task and have an open mind. She knows how to tap into your creativity, develop your talents and transform those talents into performance to help you move towards your dreams. She knows how to ask the right questions. Although she continually challenged me throughout the entire process of writing this book, I felt comfortable with the suggestions and advice she gave me. I can call on her at any time to ask questions or discuss an idea.

Our work sessions had many "environmental" teachable moments when we sat in her backyard patio with all its greenery, serenity and wildlife. During these meetings, I befriended her beloved 16 year old, long-haired cat, Angel, whose presence was often a part of our two-year writing period. Coach fed me healthy food, special teas, and with patience and a nurturing spirit, she challenged my thinking. She genuinely cares for people, family, animals, and nature and is a role model to many people. She is a constant reminder that the world is full of kind and generous people!

To this day, I am still amazed by her continued commitment and dedication. This was truly a labor of love on her part. Without her guidance, the direction and context of this project would have been very different.

PREFACE

"The purpose of our lives is to be happy."   ~ Dalai Lama

Buckle your seatbelts and get ready for an informative, thought-provoking and eye-opening perspective on the Power of Human Worth!

Today, all over the world, there is a need for an awakening to the importance of the Power of Human Worth for the well-being of us all. Just as human beings cannot realize their maximum potential without a healthy realization of their Human Worth, neither can a society be at its greatest when its members do not value themselves or others. The Power of Human Worth is an idea whose time has come.

This is a story about awareness and understanding of the Power of Human Worth, but it is also an inspiring story about my life and how I transcended difficult and painful obstacles to connect to my real self and find meaning and purpose in life. Connected to my inherent worth, I triumphed over seemingly insurmountable odds and now help others to do the same.

I have called unto God and He has answered, allowing me to accomplish things that most said I could not achieve. "Call unto me, and I will answer thee, and shew thee great and mighty things, which thou knowest not." (*Jeremiah 33:3, King James Version*)

I am a pastor without a collar, a "cop" without a badge, a psychologist without a Ph.D., and a coach without a team. This is my true life's story. I have overcome many obstacles to find happiness and fulfillment. I hope it will inspire and encourage you to overcome the obstacles in your life and take the necessary action to be all that you can be.

This book is written to motivate those who are unaware of or don't understand their true meaning and purpose. My goal is to help you understand your inherent worth and how that can help anyone live a happy life. No matter what your background is you will be able to relate to the information in this book. Like my wife wandering around the children's section of our local library in search of good books for our children's lives, you may well have been searching for a tool to better your life. I believe that this book is that tool.

A Chinese proverb says that a journey of a thousand miles begins with one step. By reading this book, you will have taken that challenging first step on a journey to find more meaning and purpose in your life.

As I travel into the wonderful world of Human Worth, I weave a tapestry with different threads and fabrics laying out my handiwork for you to view and examine how it can affect the design of your own life and an entire community. Lives can be changed for the better and for all of humanity.

I won't tell you what to think, feel or believe—nor will I perform any miracles. I'm merely going to invite you to challenge yourself to open up your mind and learn the power of your Human Worth...to strive and look within for your worth as I have.

With this book, I have taken a giant step to share my life story and show how I was able to do the "impossible." My life experiences culminated in a desire, no, a dream, to impact other people's lives by developing the power of their Human Worth. I now see my life as a beacon, a lighthouse, a ray of hope for others, especially for those of you searching for a better way to lead your lives. I would like to say with confidence and excitement that this book will help you to understand that a new reality can be yours and show you how you can connect to your Human Worth.

INTRODUCTION

"It is not how much we do, but how much love we put in the doing. It is not how much we give, but how much love we put in the giving."
~ Mother Teresa of Calcutta (1910-1997)

The teachings of some of the greatest minds on the planet had a profound impact on my beliefs and ways of thinking. These most inspiring men and women were: Jesus Christ, whom I call my true mentor and role model and who made the ultimate sacrifice; Archbishop Emeritus Desmond Tutu, my peace maker; Mother Theresa, my saint of the Inner-Cities; Nelson Mandela, my freedom fighter; His Holiness the Dalai Lama, my spiritual champion for compassion and love; Mahatma Gandhi, my father of independence and wisdom, and Rev. Dr. Martin Luther King, Jr., my drum major for justice. They used their time, talent and resources and were willing to take on causes that were greater than themselves. One attribute all these icons possess is a perception that enabled them to see more in their fellow man than the average "Joe" would ever see. Their love and compassion demonstrate their unselfish commitment to serve humanity. Their powerful life stories have inspired me to be a mentor and role model and to make a difference in the lives of others.

Over the last two decades of my life, I have shared the Power of Human Worth with everyone that has crossed my path from the White House to the inner-city, from the church to the organization, from the small business to the corporation and from the family to the individual. I have motivated, coached, counseled, advised, and encouraged people on the Power of Human Worth. This power has changed my life forever, and I've seen it change their lives as well. I have finally learned to accept myself for who I am and others as I find them. I will continue to help create and empower a body of productive citizens with the philosophy of Human Worth so that they can believe in themselves and their communities and influence others to do the same. I want to give them a vision that they will hopefully share with others.

I have met some amazing individuals who were survivors, defied the odds, overcame insurmountable obstacles and shared their life stories with me; they have become my family and friends. I have experienced the same fear, pain, worry, and stress that overwhelmed them all. As I listened to their life stories and learned from them, I became passionate about serving others. Their compelling stories impacted my life forever. They taught me about Human Worth. I have learned that it's important to treat all people with compassion and empathy because all human beings have Human Worth. Their experiences became my teachable moments where I learned that we should value all people equally; no one has less value than another, nor is anyone better than another as it relates to our Human Worth.

I've been asked by my family and friends why I continually help disadvantaged people, especially those who have lost faith and hope and struggle daily with emotional pain. My response is that every human life has Worth. Serving others first gives my own life value, importance, purpose, and meaning.

With this in mind, I have created my philosophy on the Power of Human Worth as a way to unleash the potential that we all possess. I believe Human Worth needs to be included as part of everyone's success plans and strategies for living their lives, parenting, educating, or mentoring. I am confident that this book will serve as a guide to not only finding your own "Human Worth" and transforming it into your own true potential, but will also empower our next generation of young people.

In this book you will learn to set the true price of your Worth; this is crucial because the world puts the same value on you as you put on yourself. I learned that I don't have to be perfect even though God created me perfectly with no mistakes, which means I am unique, one of a kind, and there is no one else like me. When you are overly critical or have unrealistic expectations of yourself and others, you short-change yourself. The more Self-Worth you have, the better you can determine the outcomes of your life.

In this book, I cover the following four major areas which have impacted my life in such a way that I am compelled to share them with you:

1. **Human Worth**
   Human Worth gives our lives value, meaning and purpose. Every human being has an inherent worth. It is our permanent companion from birth and the essence of who we are.

2. **Concept of Self**
   Our Self-Concept is based upon and shaped by both internal and external influences. It's a complex system of learned beliefs, attitudes and opinions that each of us holds to be true about our personal existence. It determines how

we think, feel and behave. It's how we see ourselves in regard to our Self-Esteem, Self-Worth, Self-Confidence, Self-Love, Self-Determination, Self-Respect, Self-Pride, Self-Dignity, and more.

3. Transformational Change

Change is a continuous process of re-adjusting and refining relationships and ways of acting. When we understand and accept that change is necessary to free ourselves of harmful beliefs and attitudes, we can begin the transformational process. Human Worth empowers people to change.

4. The Importance of Mentors

Mentors are instrumental in inspiring, motivating and challenging people to reach beyond their perceived limitations. Mentors can modify or change the values, beliefs and behaviors of others.

HUMAN WORTH

"To know thyself is to be true to thyself"
> ~ Socrates (c. 469/470 BC-399 BC), Greek philosopher

We learned that the sun is a star and the center of our solar system with planets revolving around it. We thought it was amazing that wherever the sun goes in space, the rest of our solar system follows! We learned that the stars produce and give off their own heat and light. But even today, we still don't know everything about the vast universe; our knowledge is only a microcosm of its infinity and endlessness. There are billions of galaxies in the universe that remain to be discovered.

So it is with ourselves in discovering who we are. Within our own worlds we will experience a lifetime of highs and lows, good and bad days, surprises and disappointments, reunions and separations, joy and pain. Isn't it then safe to say that in our lifetime we will continuously be discovering who we are?

Who am I? For millennia, philosophers, theologians, poets, artists, and others have pondered this question. Throughout our lives, we will search our mind, body and soul for this answer; this search will shape our dreams, possibilities and potentials.

What gives our lives meaning and purpose? What gives us motivation to do whatever we do? What gives us passion to achieve our wildest dreams? How do you define worth?

Worth is the foundation for all of our future endeavors. Therefore, we must take the responsibility of clarifying for ourselves and others precisely what "Human Worth" means for each of us and how and why it affects our lives as profoundly as it does.

I believe that Human Worth is a universal law that transcends any society or culture. It is also an abstract concept that has a very fragile basis in reality. Human Worth transcends the senses; although we cannot see it, we can feel its indefinable power. It's impossible to determine true Human Worth based on any one standard because the criteria are subjective and variable. It is your own internal experience, however brief and occasional it may be, that is the evidence to show that your personal worth exists[1]—what is by nature the birthright of every human being.

Where did I come from? Why in the world am I here? You were planted here as a seed of consciousness. The Scripture says, *"Let the earth bring forth grass, the herb yielding seed, and the fruit tree yielding fruit after his kind, whose seed is in itself, upon the earth: and God saw that it was so"* (Genesis 1:11, King James Version).

"In the beginning was the Word, and the Word was with God, and the Word was God,...And the Word was made flesh, and dwelt among us. . ." (John 1:1, 14). This means that the origin of life, breath, and the intellect of man began with the spoken word of God. When God speaks, life happens! And our worth starts as we emerge from our mother's womb into the outside world.

The Creator of the universe wonderfully made us and our birth was no accident. We were born with worth, and it is the most important possession we own. Our birthright is a celebration of our uniqueness in the world. At birth, the hospital registered us with an official identity recording on our birth certificate our name, birth date, nationality, and so on. Likewise, at birth, our Human Worth stamps us with value, importance and significance because we exist and are alive. Human Worth is your birthright—your entitlement to knowing that you are priceless, invaluable, precious, deserving, and worthwhile. Our birthright, unlike birthdays, needs to be celebrated everyday of the week and every month of the year, every year for the rest of our lives.

When we question our birthright, we question our right to connect to our worth. Human Worth exists, but it is equally distributed and incorruptible; everyone at birth has an equal amount of worth. No matter what happens in their life, no matter what they do or is done to them, their Human Worth cannot be diminished or increased. Nobody is worth more or less than anyone else.[2] We should not compare ourselves to others and make constant value judgments about our relative worth. To this extent, worth is an entitlement—it teaches us that we don't need permission from others to exist.

---

[1] Saundra Bubniak, *Human worth contingent on struggle to survive not cultural criteria,* http://www.examiner.com/holistic-health-in-detroit/human-worth-contingent-on-struggle-to-survive-not-cultural-criteria. Accessed Jan 2011.
[2] Ibid.

Worth is the consciousness of mind that every living human being possesses. It is that part of our character which determines our individual perception, value and importance. It is deeply rooted within us and strongly influences our attitudes and behaviors which, in turn, inevitably influence our successes or failures. It keeps us grounded in reality while allowing us to explore the potential of further development, i.e., how one can change and learn new ways of thinking which can empower oneself and influence others. Our worth is our true identity. It is the essence of who we are—who we are today and who we will become tomorrow. It's our permanent companion from birth. Human Worth is power that cannot be lost, stolen, taken by force or diminished with time.

Worth allows us to maintain, re-establish and renew our real value from the inside out—not from the outside in. It does not depend upon what we do, what we have or what anyone thinks about us. It allows us to see the goodness, usefulness and importance of ourselves and others, irrespective of public or popular opinions, financial value or social status. The Power of Human Worth helps us to avoid pride, selfishness, conceit, and arrogance.

It is not what we do for a living, have accomplished in life or what material things we possess that make us worthy. The belief that you have value as a person only when you have accomplished something or are competent in some important area is irrational. Achievement does not, except by arbitrary definition, augment your intrinsic worth. If you see yourself as a "better" or "greater" person because you succeed at something, you may temporarily feel "worthier." But your successes do not actually raise your intrinsic worth one bit, nor do your failures lower your human value. When you identify and rate your Self according to how you perform some particular activity, you create the illusion that you have only as much worth as that activity. You may achieve greater happiness or more efficiency by achieving some goal, but feeling "better off" does not make you a "better" person. You are "good," "worthwhile" or "deserving" simply because you exist, because you are alive. To raise your "ego" by achievements actually is false pride, i.e., the belief that because you have accomplishments, you have "real" value.[3]

Nor is our worth the value placed on us by others. Worth is what we see when we look in the mirror. It is the person that stares

[3]Todd Atkins, *Earning Your Worth Through Accomplishment—Human Doing Instead of Human Being,*Baton Rouge Counseling, Jun 8, 2010, http://batonrougecounseling.net/earning-worth-accomplishment-human-human/. Accessed Feb 2011.

back at us. Our worth gives us permission to not only accept what we see in the mirror, but also to embrace that individual. When asked, "Who are you?" how would you answer? "I'm a mom." "I'm a doctor." "I live in Florida." These answers are not who you are or were created to be, but what you do, what your social station is or how you see your function in life. The real, true, genuine substance of who you are is what Dr. Phil defines as the "authentic self." The authentic self is the *you* that can be found at your absolute core. It is the part of you not defined by your job, function or role. It is the composite of all your skills, talents and wisdom. It is all of the things that are uniquely yours and need expression, rather than what you believe you are supposed to be and do.[4]

Our worth can't be taken from us, nor can we lose it...but we can lose sight of it. When people lose sight of their worth, it affects us all in a negative way. When my Self-Worth was low, I found myself having little or no energy to think, feel or perform. I lacked the motivation to participate in life. We can forget we were wonderfully made by the Creator and that we are no accident. We deceive ourselves when we feel we are of no value. This is a wrong message to send to our Human Worth. Do not forget that the Creator of the universe gave us meaning, value and purpose at birth and that this birthright cannot be taken from us.

Worth is our conscience. It speaks to us throughout our lives. It defines right and wrong. It is a support system that prepares and strengthens us as we meet the challenges, pitfalls and stumbling blocks of life.

One of the true hallmarks of our Human Worth is our compassion and empathy for others. These are God-like qualities within our Human Worth that help us to open our hearts with love and respect to serve and care for those in need. Our Human Worth keeps us centered in a caring spirit. Jesus Christ, Martin Luther King, Mahatma Gandhi, Nelson Mandela, and Mother Teresa exhibited the ultimate in compassion and empathy. I call their lives "Human Worth in action." Their compassionate actions involved a resolute willingness to give of themselves for the good of others.

However, worth also gives us permission to love *ourselves* unconditionally and give priority to our *own* needs and happiness. It allows us to cultivate our inner being. It allows us to nurture our spirit, soul and body.

Our worth is the overall measure of how much we value and love ourselves. Therefore, no one but our Self is responsible for our

---

[4] Dr. Phil, *Self Matters: Defining Your Authentic Self,* http://www.drphil.com/articles/article/73. Accessed Mar 2011.

happiness and our worth. A strong sense of worth is achieved by connecting to our inner self and accepting ourselves as we are and accepting others as we find them. Believing in ourselves and our almost limitless potential is the most basic, positive belief that will give us the strength and motivation to be happy. This internal validation or acceptance is far more important to our happiness than the approval or external validation that comes from others. This requires us to confront and battle our limiting self-beliefs. We must understand that we all have limits, but we must question ourselves: Why do we retain negative thoughts, ideas and beliefs that bring us little or no happiness?

Worth is our personal, yet eternal spring of life. It is an ever-replenishing source of inner strength as we develop into who we want to become—not what others want us to be. It gives us passion, purpose and power. Our worth helps us advance and to soar and climb above any painful images and feelings that we may keep buried and hidden deep inside our souls. Our worth is built-in motivation to help us grow to our fullest potential possible. It motivates us as we seek to discover new medicines, invent new power sources or create new works of art.

Worth is our built-in survival mechanism; it gives us the strength to get up when life knocks us down. It is our shelter during the storm. It is our constant companion when we find ourselves at our lowest points. But worth also gives us permission to bend—as long as we don't allow ourselves to break—during trying times.

Worth is the internal master healer of our wounds. It is the medicine that no doctor can prescribe which heals our souls in times of trial or distress. No matter how bad things may appear, it allows us to survive tragedies, mistakes, inconveniences, or setbacks. Worth is our comfort when we are shattered by the hurt inflicted upon us by others who do not value our worth.

Our worth is constantly influenced by society. It's no secret that the media are pervasive and drive our popular culture. Television, music, videos, movies, magazines, and the internet are some of the many ways the media manipulates our thinking. They are selling a platform to make money and communicate whatever it takes to sell it and its products. In our environment, the media perpetuates negative images of violence, sexual aggression and fear; these blatant, but sometimes hidden, messages influence and misguide our behavior. They create images and trends that appeal to us in our everyday lives. They lure us to incorporate these ideals which distort our self-concept. This is especially true for the many youth who are easily influenced to conform to the latest message or trend.

In February, 2010, this dynamic was "played" upon when the enormously successful play "Wicked" came to Tampa, Florida, and was used by the educational arm of the Tampa Bay Performing Arts Center. For those who have not seen the play, suffice it to say that the script could be interpreted in the very simplest of terms as the struggle between the "good" witch and the "evil" witch, between following the lead of others (conformity) vs. believing in yourself. In the end, being true to oneself and not caving in to conformity winds up being the "right" thing to do. The Center's Patel Conservatory Performing Arts School chose to use the script as an instructive tool for developing critical thinking skills and offered a series of lessons to its students that were directly based on the "Wicked" script. The educational material acknowledged that "...students now live in a world where the media is pervasive and drives our popular culture."[5] The question-based lessons inspired students to assess their own sources of information and how they respond to the barrage of media influences that permeate their lives. These "Wicked" lessons served as an instructive tool for developing critical-thinking skills and demonstrated how important it is to "...be yourself in spite of the hidden persuaders that manipulate our way of thinking."[6]

Like a toddler who cannot run immediately, but must first learn to crawl and then walk, our Worth is developed throughout life. It cannot be truly understood or gained overnight. Sudden fame and success are mirages that will quickly fade; at best, those are illusions of our self-importance. Achieving worth is a journey and a daily exercise connecting to and learning from those positive experiences that we either obtain for ourselves or are lucky enough to receive from others.

In their 1996 research, Drs. Roy Baumeister, Laura Smart and Joseph Boden concluded that unconditional love of self and others is the best cure for violence in ourselves and society.[7] Only if we love ourselves and others unconditionally can we undermine the conditions that create violence. It is when we define ourselves by external and/or unstable conditions, such as career, financial success or others' opinions, that our worth becomes fragile. We must prioritize the value of unconditional Self-Love.[8]

---

[5] This information can no longer be referenced at http://www.patelconservatory.org/ . It was removed shortly after the show left this venue.

[6] Ibid.

[7] Roy E. Baumeister, Joseph M. Boden, and Laura Smart, *Relation of Threatened Egotism to Violence and Aggression: The Dark Side of High Self-Esteem*, American Psychological Association, Inc., 103.1 (1996): 5-33. Citation: http://www.emotionalcompetency.com/papers/baumeistersmartboden1996%5B1%5D.pdf. Accessed Jun 2010.

[8] Ibid.

We shape and define our destiny by the manner in which we view our worth in life. When Self-Worth is at a high level, people can believe their personal efforts will make a difference wherever or whenever they become involved in society. This high Self-Worth results in a confidence that is perceived by others and inevitably increases chances for success.

Billions of people have walked and lived upon this planet, all sharing the same conditions of mortality; we all suffer and we all die. But not one can do what you do, say what you say or go where you go. Each individual human life has an immeasurable value and has something unique and irreplaceable to offer to the greater whole of society. We must learn to appreciate the beautiful qualities we possess. In my experience, the responsibility and solution to connecting to our Human Worth starts with accepting ourselves as we are. We should strive to accept who we are and, in turn, encourage others to recognize their own uniqueness and distinctive worth.

Can we really know who we are? What gets us up in the morning? What inspires us? With our fast-paced lifestyles, we find it difficult to stop long enough to be calm, still or to silence our minds in order to connect to our real self. We are constantly on the go in search of unrealistic, unreachable dreams and ideals at any price—even at the expense of who we are. We push our minds, bodies and souls to the limit. We go through the same routines and motions every day; yet, too often, we are not happy or satisfied. It's a long and rocky road to the recovery of one's total worth.

We will not truly understand who we are until we make a conscious effort to think and behave in ways that help us value ourselves and place a priority on what gives our lives meaning and purpose. We all have a positive and negative image of ourselves; the question becomes, "Which side will you allow to control you?" Very few individuals are able to completely realize their full human potential during their lifetime. By awakening the untapped human potential that exists within us, we can reduce the frustrations in our lives and improve the relationships which jeopardize our worth.

Socrates is famous for arguing that we must "Know Thyself" to be wise, that the un-examined life is not worth living. Reflecting on our lives will lead to the realization that the person in the mirror truly exists inside our head, heart and spirit.

Before we take any steps in finding out who we are, we need to understand the Concept of Self which is key to understanding our Human Worth and improving the quality of our lives.

"The most basic of all human needs is to understand and to be understood."

~ Dr. Ralph G. Nichols (1907-2005)[9]

It's time to remove the façade and uncover the real you. See your own inherent value and importance—accept and embrace it. Be realistic in your view of your Self—your weaknesses and your strengths, your limitations and your potential—and you will see the world in a different light—not as a bad place, but with hope and the opportunities to become all that you want to be.

---

[9] Dr. Ralph G. Nichols, professor of rhetoric and expert in the field of listening, served for decades as the Chairman of the Department of Rhetoric, Univ. of Minnesota. His 1948 Doctoral Dissertation at the Univ. of Iowa identified the groundbreaking factors that differentiated the behaviors of effective and ineffective listeners, which established a benchmark for future listening scholars and practitioners.

THE CONCEPT OF SELF

T he Concept of Self plays a key role in our perception of our quality of life and well-being. There is growing awareness that of all the perceptions we experience in the course of living, none has more profound significance than the perceptions we hold regarding our own personal existence—our concept of who we are and how we fit into the world.

The Concept of Self may be defined as a complex system of learned beliefs, attitudes and opinions that each of us holds to be true about our personal existence. Erich Fromm said it beautifully when he described the Concept of Self as "life being aware of itself." This awareness is part of what makes human experience unique and precious, but it also leads to problems. If you realize you exist as a distinct person, a thing apart, then you can also feel separateness and loneliness.[10]

The Concept of Self includes *Self-Esteem, Self-Worth, Self-Confidence, Self-Love, Self-Determination, Self-Respect, Self-Pride, Self-Dignity,* and more. It affects our attitudes and behaviors which, in turn, determine our successes or failures and has a very strong impact on our happiness. It comes from the knowledge we accumulate every day about ourselves and how we evaluate ourselves. This knowledge helps us to evaluate our physical, moral, personal, and social selves and is based upon and shaped by both internal and external influences. It determines how we think, feel and behave.

How we think about or evaluate ourselves is critical to our Concept of Self. It becomes our identity, ego and psyche. Franken states, *"there is a great deal of research which shows that the*

---

[10] Erich Fromm (1900-1980), American psychologist. *The Art of Loving* (1956) is his best known work. Citation: Russell A. Dewey, *Psychology: An Introduction,* http://www.psywww.com/intropsych/ch16_sfl/art_of_loving.html. Accessed Apr 10, 2011.

[concept of self] is, perhaps, the basis for all motivated behavior. It is the [concept of self] that gives rise to possible selves, and it is possible selves that create the motivation for behavior." [11]

Our Concept of Self is dynamic. To understand its active nature, imagine it as a gyrocompass: a continuously active system that dependably points to the "true north" of our perceived existence. This guidance system not only shapes the way we view ourselves, others and the world, but it also serves to direct our behavior and action and provides consistency in our personality. Our Self's gyrocompass enables us to take a consistent stance in life.

We develop and maintain our Concept of Self through the process of taking action and then reflecting on what we have done and what others tell us about what we have done. It is important that we reflect on these different aspects of our Self because we perceive them (Self-Love, Self-Pride, etc.) with varying degrees of clarity at different times. This reflection is based on actual and possible actions in comparison to one's own expectations and the expectations of others and to the characteristics and accomplishments of others.[12] That is, the Concept of Self is not innate, but is constructed and developed by the individual through interaction with the environment and reflecting on that interaction. This dynamic aspect of the self-concept is important because it indicates that it can be modified or changed.

As far as we know, no one is born with a Concept of Self. Infants do not have a Concept of Self because it doesn't yet exist for them. Infants behave as if they are the center of the universe and everything in it is there for their own pleasure and satisfaction. They do not make any negative judgment about themselves. Their Concept of Self gradually emerges in the early months of life and is shaped and reshaped through experiences and interactions with others and the environment.

The fact that our self-concept is learned has some important implications. Karl Marx was right when he said, *"We are shaped by our environment. Whether we wish it or not we are susceptible to the labels and whims of society. We are forced to fall under the eye of our peers on a daily basis, and though it may no longer be a*

---

[11]Robert E. Franken, *Human Motivation*, 3rd ed. (Pacific Grove, CA: Brooks/Cole, 1994), p 443. Citation: W. Huitt, *Self and Self-Views*, Educational Psychology Interactive, 2009, Valdosta, GA: Valdosta State Univ., http://www.edpsycinteractive.org/topics/self/self.html. Accessed Nov 2010.
[12] W. Huitt, *Self and Self-Views*, Educational Psychology Interactive, 2009, Valdosta, GA: Valdosta State Univ., http://www.edpsycinteractive.org/topics/self/self.html. Accessed Nov 2010.

conscious thought, we are always thinking at the back of our minds...who am I going to be today?"[13]

Sometimes, we camouflage ourselves and put on a false face at work, school, church, around friends and family pretending that we're happy when we are really sad. We hide behind masks to dance around the fact that we don't want to reveal what is really on our minds. We are destined to hide behind our masks for the rest of our lives if we don't learn to accept ourselves.

Many of us live a fast-paced lifestyle constantly on the go in search of unrealistic, unreachable dreams and ideals at any price— even at the expense of who we are. Every day we wake up and look in the mirror, but do we see who we truly are?

How do you perceive yourself? How do you feel about yourself? It is imperative to learn to stop long enough to calm your mind, go within yourself, become aware of your feelings, thoughts and deeds, and then to accept them. In order for our Worth to come shining through, we must avoid becoming overly stressed, tired or worried. A negative Concept of Self can make us feel lonely, isolated, disenchanted and complacent with our lives. Despite a poor Concept of Self, our Human Worth will inspire us to take pleasure, pride and satisfaction in all that we accomplish in our lives. A positive Concept of Self has a strong impact on our feelings of happiness and contentment. We need time in our lives to discover and reflect on who our real Self is.

There are two powerful things that impact everyone's Concept of Self. The first is one's own opinion and judgment of themselves (internal influence). The second important influence on our Concept of Self is our "interpretation" of other's perceptions of us (external influence).

By working towards creating a positive view and image of ourselves, we strengthen our self-concept and increase our potential to succeed in life. We need to recognize our positive traits or else we will struggle with our Human Worth.

In our external environment, people are constantly evaluating us and offering opinions, views, judgments, and suggestions. Our immediate families may give us love, inspiration and encouragement to do the best we can. Their love may be very important to us. How people view us and behave towards us may add to or detract from our Concept of Self and has a profound impact on the image we have of ourselves. However, they seldom

---

[13] W. Oostvee, *Concept of Self: An Introduction,* (n.d.), http://chat.carleton.ca/~wvoostve/secondpro/pwrlife.htm. Accessed Apr 2011.

take the time to understand our hurt or pain, our goals in life, our fears, our dreams. They do not realize that their advice may actually block our potential by negatively altering our Concept of Self. The opinions others have of us are valuable feedback for us to understand how we see ourselves, but they don't impact or determine our inherent Human Worth which we are born with. Internal validation of who we are (our Human Worth) will always trump external validation. Therefore, accepting their suggestions to our problems when they don't truly understand our hurt, pain, fear, dreams, and goals can block or limit our true potential.

How well do you know yourself? Trying to learn who we are in this vast and complex world is not very easy. It is valuable and important to have knowledge of your abilities, skills, talents, and beliefs because it deeply affects your Concept of Self and ultimately your Human Worth. To better understand your Concept of Self, who you are, you need to reflect in a variety of ways about your existence here on earth: philosophically, culturally, psychologically, religiously, symbolically, etc.

During my childhood years, the information I learned about myself was both good and bad. I had little control of the influences in and around my life, so much of my self-image as a child was a reflection of the perception others held about me. The Concept of Self that emerged was one that was "other–oriented," based on the opinions of others, instead of being based on my own inherent importance and value as a human being.

The Thomaston Years

I was born into a poor family in the tiny rural farming community of Thomaston, Alabama, in 1963. Most of the people who lived in Thomaston were descendants of black slaves brought in to pick cotton on the large plantations when cotton was king. Like other rural areas throughout Alabama, Thomaston existed as a reminder of the traditional rural life in Alabama—rural poverty with age-old patterns of living and thinking while resisting modern change. Can you imagine living in the 1960's without running water in your home and having to use an outhouse? I did.

I was the seventeenth of twenty-one children born to my mother, Maxine. My mother bore a total of 11 boys, 4 girls and 6 stillborns. She had her first child when she was approximately 14 years old. When I was born, I already had 8 brothers and 3 sisters, the eldest being 18 years old. I never knew my biological father, even to this day. My mother, affectionately known as Madear, met our basic needs and loved us unconditionally to the best of her ability as she struggled with her own personal issues and problems.

My family didn't have the money to buy nice things like some families in my neighborhood. I spent the first eight years of my life living in a three-room shotgun house without indoor plumbing or running water. My family had to carry water by the buckets from a pipe on the hill that supplied water for the horses. I fetched drinking water from the hill every day after school. This water was poured into washtubs for baths and kept in containers for drinking. But I never knew we were poor, and I grew up playful without a care in the world—my life was simple.

Madear receives a thank you kiss from James

In Cat's Alley, the section of Thomaston where I lived, everyone bartered and shared within their extended families and lived a simple way of life. My relatives grew small crops like peanuts, corn and greens and also raised chickens, hogs, and goats. During the day, I could visit any of my relatives to share a meal. In addition, I remember my family receiving free government commodities—cans of peanut butter, packages of cheese and large sacks of grits. My older brothers and uncles would work on nearby farms to earn money, and my mother would travel to the nearby town of Linden[14] to clean houses for small wages to provide necessities for our large family. At times, she would even pick cotton in nearby fields to earn more money.

Occasionally, on a Saturday night, a drunken uncle would be fished out of the river when he fell off the footbridge, putting smiles on the faces of all those watching. Laughter and humor were everywhere you turned. Large family gatherings to celebrate the holidays were fun times for all. These were always outdoor affairs with different family members contributing whatever they raised on their land. Since everyone shared, I never realized we were poor—until I moved away from Thomaston. After experiencing the freedom of the outdoors, the only downside to

---

[14] Linden is a traditional small town with Southern charm and hospitality and serves as the County seat for Marengo County. It is strategically located in West Central Alabama where U.S. Hwy 43 and Alabama Hwy 69 and 28 intersect.

my early childhood was going to school. I did not want to remain inside all day; I wanted to be back on the farm with the animals. I wanted to run with the horses instead of having to sit still in a seat all day. In my family, education was not important; most family members dropped out of school.

Our community was like the television sitcom "Cheers" where everybody knew your name and shared resources no matter your money status, where you lived or what class you came from. Thomaston people were genuine, strong and hard-working. During the harvest season I remember my family and relatives sharing their crops and hunting with one another. A meal could be had at any time whether at grandpa's, an aunt's or a cousin's house. I grew up during a time when people cared about others, there were community gatherings, one church served the needs of our community, and a people's word was their bond.

The simplicity of my childhood in Thomaston enabled me to appreciate the simple, authentic things in life—spiritual music (having grown up attending a small church on the hill), running with horses in a wide open pasture, the serenity of sitting on a riverbank fishing with a cane pole, the pleasure of the cool breeze that blows off a river, being surrounded by colorful wildflowers, and the smell of green grass. The lessons I learned were about belonging, caring for others, being genuine, and treating people as valuable in themselves, not for what they can do for you.

Whatever anxieties the adults may have been experiencing were not felt by us children. I remember love and serenity. I knew that I was loved by my mother, relatives and community. My mother shaped my moral character and instilled in me a sense of self-worth that gave me real hope for the future. The integrity of my relatives helped shaped my attitude and influenced my passion for helping others. My grandfather, Clark Cade, represented the strong father-figure for both his extended family and the entire neighborhood.

Overall, my early life growing up in the country awakened my tender feelings of affection and gave me comfort. It was the place where I felt secure and allowed to be myself. The amount of wealth or property was not important. My family earned a living with their hands in the fields. Again, life was simple. My concept of Self was happy and joyful.

But then came some hurdles that challenged my peaceful childhood and caused my life to change. First, my younger brother, Lucas, died in my mother's arms when, as a baby, his heart suddenly seized. A few years later my older brother Phillip took ill and had to be hospitalized in Mobile, Alabama, for an extensive period. One of my older brothers convinced my mom to move the family to Prichard to be near Phillip. At that point, everything in our lives changed, but I didn't have a clue as to how drastically my Concept of Self would change. I was about to discover how my new environment would impact my sense of Self–Esteem.

Now, let's take a look at some of the basic elements of your own unique SELF...starting with your Self-Worth.

Self-Worth

"Your living is determined not so much by what life brings to you as by the attitude you bring to life; not so much by what happens to you as by the way your mind looks at what happens." ~ Kahlil Gibran

Self-Worth is how much we value and love ourselves and is based on our current knowledge about ourselves. While *Human Worth* is our permanent birthright and is always with us, *Self-Worth* changes as we encounter new experiences and challenges. Self-Worth is a feeling that we can cultivate in order to have Self-Confidence and Self-Esteem.

What makes people worthwhile? Where do you look for evidence of worth? What are the criteria? It may help somewhat to remind yourself that every criterion ever devised for measuring worth is dependent on its cultural context. The Zen monk of great virtue is perceived as worthless on Wall Street. The highly respected stockbroker is perceived as worthless in the jungles of the Amazon. The most powerful Indian medicine man is perceived as worthless in the halls of Congress.[15] Our inherent Human Worth cannot be measured by our achievements or successes or how we compare to others. The true measure of our Human Worth is the value we place on ourselves, not the value that the world would measure us by.

In our culture, we too often equate worth with work. Some believe that you are what you do, and that other positions and professions are more or less worthy than yours. For example, doctors are better than psychologists, who are better than lawyers, who are better than accountants, who are better than stockbrokers, who are better than hardware clerks, and so forth. Within a given profession or social status, our culture awards worth based on accomplishments. Getting a raise, a degree, a promotion, or winning a competition is worth a great deal. Acquiring the right house, car, furnishings, boat, or college education for your kids are all accomplishments that are worth a lot. However, if you get fired or laid off, lose your home or in any other way slip down the

---

[15] Saundra Bubniak, *Human worth contingent on struggle to survive not cultural criteria,* http://www.examiner.com/holistic-health-in-detroit/human-worth-contingent-on-struggle-to-survive-not-cultural-criteria. Accessed Jan 2011.

accomplishment ladder, you become socially worthless. If an employee equates his worth with accomplishment and is late in meeting an important deadline, s/he may feel inadequate and worthless. Feeling worthless, s/he may become depressed. Being depressed, s/he may work more slowly and miss more deadlines. This can be a deadly downward spiral.[16]

For many of us, our sense of self-worth becomes firmly and dangerously entwined in our estimation of our *net* worth. When we limit our definition of self-worth to our net worth or equate worth to work, results can be devastating or even deadly. This was powerfully illustrated by the alarming increase in white-collar suicides since the onset of the recent economic recession. There was a rise in the premeditated deaths of people who lost significant amounts of money and strongly associated their net worth with their personal value as human beings. Suicide notes and follow-up conversations with the affected families revealed the despair and demoralization the now deceased individuals had suffered as a result of no longer having financial wealth. They found life unbearable. This describes a very sad state of affairs in our culture.[17]

Our financial portfolios, the size of our homes and the number and quality of our possessions certainly factor into our sense of personal wealth. But in determining that personal wealth, we should place at least as much weight (and hopefully more) on other assets, such as our health and well-being, the quality of our relationships and our ability to find happiness and enjoy life more.[18]

Our minds are full of outdated concepts, unexamined feelings and unrealistic fears and fantasies of who we are and where we are going. We see the world from the perspective of approval vs. disapproval or acceptance vs. rejection. We are not worth less just because we don't have a six-figure income, a PhD or live in a gated community with a beautiful home with a white picket fence, a perfect spouse and 2.1 children. We need to spring-clean our minds and discard what we don't need. We must develop a positive image of ourselves that is not based on external values. These material things are only to impress others and fit into socially-accepted norms; they do not determine where we are going as it relates to our Human Worth.

---

[16]Ibid.
[17]Goldberg, Steve and Barbara Goldberg. *Finding the Upside: Practical Wisdom for Challenging Times*, www.findingtheupside.org. Citation: Steve Goldberg, *When Net Worth Becomes Self-Worth*, Life As a Human: The Online Magazine for Evolving Minds, Feb 22, 2011. http://lifeasahuman.com/2011/mind-spirit/inspirational/when-net-worth-becomes-self-worth/. Accessed Mar 2011.
[18] Ibid.

"Don't let what you are doing get in the way of who you truly are."
~ James A. Ray, psychologist/therapist

To empower your Self-Worth, be completely honest with yourself—even when it means facing the worst truths about yourself. In one sense this approach has some merit; when we better understand our dysfunctional parts, we can give more control to the healthy parts of ourselves. When we deny the undesirable parts of ourselves hoping they will go away, it can cause havoc on our worth because it may create fear and anxiety. Acknowledge your worth and learn to develop trust in your abilities to be able to do what you desire and wish for. Do not allow anyone to have power over you or control you—become unstoppable!

In most instances, we are our own worst critics. We are harder on ourselves than we realize. Despite a high level of accomplishment, some people still suffer from low Self-Worth.[19] Sometimes, we expect more from ourselves, or allow others to expect more, than we can deliver. We doubt our abilities more than others do. We must keep in mind that we are not "super humans" and cannot do all things. We must accept that we all have limitations, and we're doing the best that we can with what we have. When we impose unrealistic expectations on ourselves, experience unnecessary anxiety and fail or fall short of achieving our goals or dreams, we feel guilty and worthless.

Without Self-Worth we give others permission to mold us into who *they* think we should be. Time and time again, we continually sacrifice who we are in the name of acceptance. People stay in relationships because they don't want to fail in the eyes of others, they spend more than they earn trying to keep up with the Joneses and impress others, and so on. The bottom line is that we live a lie. We've got one foot on the brake, one on the accelerator, burning rubber, and we are going nowhere. The confident driver knows when and how to step on the accelerator; a worker feeling dissatisfied in a non-fulfilling 9-5 job is braking and going nowhere.

A strong Self-Worth gives us the power to overcome fears or illusions of not being good enough. Nothing outside of you can bring you true fulfillment. Having a sense of Self-Worth allows you to access the transcendent Human Worth that already exists within you and gives your life meaning and purpose.

---

[19] Saundra Bubniak, *Human worth contingent on struggle to survive not cultural criteria*, http://www.examiner.com/holistic-health-in-detroit/human-worth-contingent-on-struggle-to-survive-not-cultural-criteria. Accessed Jan 2011.

When we suffer setbacks and inconveniences, a low Self-Worth may cause us to feel inadequate and that we will fail. This is how external influences can play on our psyche to diminish our Self-Worth (how we value ourselves). We feel "worthless" and "fragile," i.e., less worthy. Some research has shown that "Fragile Egoism" is a cause of aggressive and violent behavior.[20] As mentioned previously, when one defines oneself by external conditions, such as financial successes, educational experiences or the opinions of others, that belief increases one's fragility *because these conditions are so unstable.* The research concluded that "people who hold inflated, unstable, or tentative beliefs in the self's superiority are most likely to be 1) easily and frequently threatened by negative feedback from others, and 2) prone to react aggressively and violently to those threats. People who are dependent upon other people's approval will have an increased propensity toward violence."[21]

The authors also discuss how one's belief in a "culture of honor" and a threatened public image (such as "losing face") can foster violent responses when those beliefs are threatened. For example, a gang member may want to be seen as a "bad ass." If someone else claims he's "badder," then the only choice is to fight or be publicly humiliated. The fear of public humiliation and loss of Self-Worth seems to be worse than violence or the fear of death. When their imagined badge of honor is threatened, they resort to physical, aggressive behavior.[22]

The same thing happens to the person prone to thirst for truth and knowledge—if it leads to the belief that "I know more than most others." From someone else's perspective, I'm just a "know-it-all." Whenever we allow ourselves to get too proud in some knowledge area and our beliefs are challenged or threatened, we too may become defensive and argumentative.[23]

Fragile self-beliefs are easily threatened by anyone. When someone believes he or she must be "the best" to be "OK," that belief inherently creates a "fragile ego" because *only one* person can be the best. Only if we value ourselves and define our essential natures by more stable measures can we overcome this fragility.[24] Valuing ourselves and others undermines the conditions that

---

[20] Roy E. Baumeister, Joseph M. Boden, and Laura Smart, "Relation of Threatened Egotism to Violence and Aggression: The Dark Side of High Self-Esteem," *American Psychological Association, Inc.*, 103.1 (1996): 6. Citation: http://www.emotionalcompetency.com/papers/baumeistersmartboden1996%5B1%5D.pdf. Accessed Jun 2010.
[21] Ibid.
[22] Ibid.
[23] Ibid.
[24] Ibid.

create violence. Promoting a strong and positive Self-Worth in at-risk youth is the best cure for youth violence in our society.

In resolving or working out their predicaments or dilemmas, it is in the nature of *animals* to resort to primitive, violent behavior, but *humans* can resort to reason. When we resort to violence, we tell ourselves that we do not have a solution to the problem. Non-violence is the answer that must be communicated to the troubled youths in our communities. They need to be made aware that they have something important to say no matter what others think. Sadly, it will remain unsaid until they can establish their Self-Worth.

Breaking the Glass Ceiling

I attended elementary school on a regular basis, but there was little expectation I would ever grasp the concept of learning. The school officials labeled me as "educationally mentally retarded" with a behavior disorder. The teachers seemed to think that my future was already determined and that I would not amount to anything. This negative expectation affected my young and fragile ego, and I began to accept what I was told as reality. My mother, who had a third grade education, did not know enough to fight for my future. If you tell a person something repeatedly, eventually that person will believe it. The constant mental beating continued to cause a downward spiral in my life. No one took the time to look into my background to determine what was going on to distract me from learning. I was simply bored with school. My self-worth plummeted, and I soon believed that I would never amount to anything.

My teachers continued with the social promotions but did not try to assist me. I didn't know who I could turn to for help or who I could talk to. My stepfather, who would eventually drink himself to death, was not one I could turn to for guidance. I had far more detractors than role models.

I have always been a believer that God is always in the plan. He has a way of placing us in dire circumstances—to save those who can be saved. There were some teachers whom I feel genuinely cared about my future; but, for whatever reason, did not take me under their wings. It is possible that they had been on the battlefield for so long that they were too tired to spend the time to find out more about my problems. They didn't know that my inspiration was the Dallas Cowboys, who advertised themselves as "America's Team." They became my most influential role models at this important, impressionable stage in my life. My new-found passion was to become a professional player. I would lie in my bed at night envisioning myself playing for the Dallas Cowboys. I had a dream.

Luckily, when I entered middle school, a coach saw something in me that had been invisible to the others before him. He saw potential. Coach George Walker took me *under his wing and introduced me to athletics. Playing football was not without a price because, in order to remain on the team, I had to keep my grades above a certain level. Coach Walker did not know it at the time, but, when he "adopted" me, he introduced me to Hope. It was Hope that allowed me to turn my back on drugs and alcohol. He introduced me to a world that offered me a better life. It was this foundation that I began to build on.*

Though others helped me when they saw that I was trying to help myself, Coach Walker was the individual who placed the brick in my hand that allowed me to shatter the glass ceiling. For many inner-city youth, sports are a way out of poverty and many families sacrificed their children in the gladiator's arena in the hope of a better life. Coach never told me that my struggle would be easy. He simply showed me that my goals were attainable and that success was worth the struggle.

I encourage youths to have a sense of Self-Worth because it has a critical impact on their level of achievement. When we have unhealthy thought patterns or other self-destructive behaviors, we tend to buy into the self-fulfilling prophecy—"I'm no good, so I'll behave badly because that is what is expected of me." We cannot blame others or give others permission to hurt our feelings, frighten us or make us angry. If we choose to do so, then we become victims of our own emotions. Know your rights and enforce them—learn to say "No!" You have the right to say: "I don't know," or "I don't understand," or even, "I don't care." You have the right to make mistakes. You have the right to change your mind. It is time to stop having this self-defeating attitude and value your Human Worth.

The Self-Worth of the at-risk youth and their parents in my community is constantly being drained by social issues that result from poverty and a lack of education—a poverty that is, all too often, too great to overcome. What others in their community do and say has a major controlling effect upon them. We are social creatures and much of our orientation and validation comes from social contact. Consequently, these youth and parents mirror the low Human Worth that is reflected by their impoverished community.

Therefore, it is vital to actively choose to surround yourself with worthwhile individuals. Unworthy people must be avoided because they will drag you down and make YOU feel worthless! This avoidance is not a matter of ego or whim—this is a matter of survival. I encourage people to avoid those who "put down" or abuse them or otherwise depress and sadden them. Loneliness can be overcome in time, but a bad relationship can drag on indefinitely and limit chances of gaining better relationships. A valid relationship is one that is mutual and can provide the vital emotional support needed to enhance and encourage our worth.

I am reminded of a story of how the impact of education can be at fault in destroying the Self-Worth of our young people. After each year of learning, students were given tests which studies have now shown were inherently biased culturally and socially. For example, the following questions were asked in the first grade, "Where do you put the cup? On the table or the saucer?" The minority students replied, "on the table" which was graded as the "wrong" answer. In the second grade they were asked, "Which one do you wear when it's cold? A glove or a mitten?" The minority students replied, "A glove." Again, it was graded as the "wrong" answer. In the third grade, "Which one do you take to the beach? A bucket or a pail?" They replied, "bucket" and, again, it was graded as the "wrong" answer. The minority students had simply never been taught what a "saucer" is, so to them, a cup would instead clearly be placed "on the table." They didn't answer a "mitten" or a "pail" because in their terminology, it is only known, respectively, as a "glove" or a "bucket." Because they were unfamiliar with the terms and language of society at large, their answers were deemed "unacceptable" and graded "incorrect" due to cultural bias.

Social and cultural biases have been proven to exist in educational settings. By the time many minority children have reached the fourth grade, they start "acting out," misbehaving and shutting down. They feel that they are misunderstood and their confidence begins to deteriorate, diminishing their sense of Self-Worth. They feel out of place and inadequate because they cannot relate to what is being taught.

It gets worse….even when they go home, there is no, or, at best, limited support structure. Parents and grandparents, suffering from low Self-Worth and a lack of education themselves, impose more hardship by belittling the frustrated child telling them that they are stupid, dumb and will not amount to anything. They put the blame on the child whose feelings of worthlessness are thereby reinforced. So, not only is their Self-Worth altered by a negative educational experience that does not give them the needed personalized attention and support in the classroom, but it is also further damaged by their very own families. They struggle with loving themselves unconditionally because of the humiliation and belittlement they experience in both the home and the external environment.

In my community, Faith is a key component for the development of our Self-Worth and fulfilling our potential. Many in my community use religion and cling to the hope that their suffering will end in the next life. Some churches and mega-churches are filled with worshippers who are seeking salvation and believing they will be "done with the troubles of this old world." But many people today lack faith—they appear to be turning their backs on God and family. They are confused and feel a void in their faith. Why? Too often, it is because they feel betrayed by those they have trusted, but who have let them down. Sometimes, they are exploited for material gains by their own ministers who prey upon their vulnerabilities and lack of Self-Worth.

Lack of faith can diminish the value they place on themselves and is one underlying cause for a lack of hope, motivation and dreams. It is evidenced by the violence in our schools, the unacceptable school dropout rate and the high drug usage in our communities. Lacking faith, people feel hopeless to overcome obstacles. Their daily bout with uncertainty, insecurity, rejection, loneliness, and separation exiles them to an island of low Self-Worth. Lacking Godly principles, we create negative circumstances that complicate our lives. Negative attention is better than no attention at all. Many are more concerned with appearances and possessions than with spiritual development. Herein lies the desperate need to understand what is our Self-Worth. Self-Worth replenishes the void and confusion that so many struggle with. Faith provides us with the guidelines and boundaries that will allow us to act according to moral principles. Belief in something greater than ourselves will allow us to discover the unlimited potential we all possess. God is involved in everything we do; therefore, everything we do can be done with passion, enthusiasm, faith, and excellence. God deserves our absolute best.

Self-Esteem

"What lies behind us and what lies before us are tiny matters compared to what lies within us." ~ Ralph Waldo Emerson

When I moved from the country to the city, I was forced to leave behind a peaceful state of being and my beloved extended family members and close friends in exchange for the hustle and bustle of a chaotic city life. The change was devastating to me and my Self-Esteem.

The term Self-Esteem comes from the words "self" and "esteem." Esteem is a fancy word for thinking that someone or something is important or for valuing that person or thing. "Self" means, well, yourself! Self-Esteem is a basic human need and is indispensable to normal and healthy self-development and has a value for survival.[25] Self-Esteem reflects a person's overall evaluation or appraisal of his or her own worth. It's how you see and feel about yourself, that is, your emotional aspect of Self or how you value yourself (one's Self-Worth).

An "I gotta be me" attitude is a prerequisite for Self-Esteem. It's an assertive attitude that means we have the right: to hold and express our own feelings, thoughts and opinions, to be our own judges, to control our own lives, to be treated with respect and to be taken seriously, to err and to change our mind. We also have the right, like any human, to *not* be perfect and *not* care about being liked by everyone. In simple terms, it means that we know who we are and don't seek the approval of others.

"I gotta be me" allows us to cast off all of the unrealistic beliefs attached to our emotions about who we are. It allows us to discard false images of who others think we should be. When we do not acknowledge who we really are, any attempts we make to achieve happiness will elude us. Our country's Declaration of Independence gives us the right to life, liberty and the pursuit of happiness, but we are often frustrated by what we think should make us happy. I don't have to take a trip around the world or own a yacht to find happiness. I find it in the little things, like being on my patio overlooking a pond and observing the wildlife, the hawks and ospreys, the turtles and alligators. The American dream leads us into a frantic chase for success and prosperity, but if we don't know who we really are (i.e., are not connected to our inherent worth), then we cannot make ourselves happy. That's why "I gotta be me" to be really happy.

"I gotta be me" simply reinforces and complements our worth. It allows us to be real, authentic, genuine, and accept ourselves at face value. It means that we have recognized and mastered our God-given talents and abilities.

"I gotta be me" also means encouraging ourselves to be ourselves. It means that we can coexist and complement each other as human beings as we unconsciously project images of ourselves that affect those around us.

When we do not accept ourselves and buy into beliefs that we are ugly, different, abnormal, imperfect, or defective, our self-image is the main problem—not our actual physical appearance or mentality. We may even admit to ourselves that sometimes we talk too much, do dumb things, have not met career goals, or bore people. We may feel guilty about these negative aspects. To the degree that we do not like or accept some part of ourselves, then

[25]Nathaniel Branden, *The Psychology of Self-Esteem* (San Francisco, CA: Jossey-Bass, 2001).

our Self-Esteem will also be affected.[26] We are all only human and do things that are dysfunctional to our health and happiness. Dysfunctional habits keep us from being happy.

Psychologists usually regard Self-Esteem as an enduring personality characteristic or trait synonymous with self-regard, self-respect, self-integrity, and self-love. "...[Self-Esteem] is being competent to cope with the basic challenges of life and being worthy of happiness. Self-Esteem is a concept of personality....for it to grow, we need to have self-worth..."[27]

How our parents, relatives and friends love, nurture and influence our lives has a significant impact on our Self-Esteem. This explains why, when a family member who has raised, nurtured and loved us dies or is left behind, we feel a part of us is also gone.

However, the way we view ourselves is so often different from the way others see us. Contrary to popular belief, Self-Esteem does *not* depend on the perspectives others have of us, the kind of job we have, the car we drive, the amount of money we have in the bank, the restaurants that we dine in or the clothes that we wear. Self-Esteem depends on the opinion we have of ourselves. One psychologist suggests that "people who know themselves can maximize outcomes because they know what they can and cannot do."[28]

Because Self-Esteem is a feeling—not a skill—it can only be measured by observing the way in which a person acts or behaves. Self-Esteem determines whether or not new situations are approached in a positive and confident manner or in a negative and fearful way. It helps us to keep things in perspective whether a situation is positively or negatively charged. Self-Esteem is having the satisfaction of knowing that you are accepted, connected, unique, powerful, and capable.

"A man is but the product of his thoughts; what he thinks, he becomes."
~ Mahatma Gandhi

Self-Esteem encompasses beliefs (for example, "I am competent" or "I am incompetent") and emotions (such as triumph, despair, pride, or shame) which are reflected in a person's behavior. For example, if people feel victorious they will behave confidently.

---

[26]Ibid.
[27]Ibid.
[28]Robert E. Franken, *Human Motivation*, 3rd ed. (Pacific Grove, CA: Brooks/Cole, 1994), p 439. Citation: W. Huitt, *Self and Self-Views*, Educational Psychology Interactive, 2009, Valdosta, GA: Valdosta State Univ., http://www.edpsycinteractive.org/topics/self/self.html. Accessed Nov 2010.

Like most kids, I believed that my physical appearance was lacking; as early as the second grade, I was suspended from school because I threatened another student after he made others laugh at how I looked and told me I was ugly.

Physical appearance is emphasized so much in our society that we may become very sensitive about our image believing that it does not measure up to the ideal. The media creates negative images emphasizing sexuality and violence. Videos and lyrics imply that teens, especially females, should be free to expose greater amounts of their skin. Girls as young as 13 increasingly add to the amount of younger pregnancies because of such effective media influence. Not only is the media encouraging greater sexual promiscuity, they are influential to the degradation of women.

The time has come for us to cast out those things that make us question our physical image. We must understand that not everyone fits the popular image of beauty. Outward beauty is fleeting and can be here today and gone tomorrow. We must realize that while we may not be as outwardly attractive as another, the outward package does not always reflect the inner beauty. If an outwardly beautiful person suffers an injury that changes his appearance, does that change that person's inner-self? That person's inner-self can only be changed with their permission. It is not an automatic event that takes place because outward beauty changes. True beauty lies within ourselves.

We must learn to accept our physical limitations—to accept those images we see in the mirror—and see and appreciate our inherent beauty. We need to change the way we feel about our bodies and view ourselves through a new and more compassionate looking glass. This will not only increase our Self-Esteem but will also improve our chances to survive life's adversities.

When I was in college and the NFL, exercising daily and training year round, I developed my body into a physical specimen—the kind of body that coaches and teams wanted and what society placed importance and value on. Therefore, it was what I cared about the most, so it became my Concept of Self. I allowed my self-image, Self-Esteem, Self-Worth, and Self-Respect to be defined only by my physical body and appearance. The screaming fans reinforced and affirmed my distorted Concept of Self that was based only on being a skilled athlete. They admired and flattered me, sought out my company, listened attentively and agreed with everything I said. Society reinforced the gladiator image of an athlete.

My physical abilities compensated for my inadequacies and shortcomings in other areas and gave me importance and value. I didn't have the knowledge to understand that my *real* Self transcended how others viewed me on and off the field and what I accomplished in sports. I had developed a very positive image of myself—but it was only an illusion. It was not the *real* me—I had put the *real* me on the back burner. Today, I understand that my high Self-Esteem was built purely on external influences and would only last as long as the applause continued.

People with low Self-Esteem will consistently communicate self-derogatory statements, exhibit helplessness, not volunteer, and are overly dependent. They also demonstrate an excessive need for acceptance (especially from authority figures), practice perfectionism, have difficulty making decisions, and exhibit a low frustration tolerance. They become defensive, have little faith in their own judgment and are highly vulnerable to peer pressure. Low Self-Esteem makes one vulnerable to failure. If you suffer from low Self-Esteem and feel like you are not worth anything, take a good long look at yourself through the lens of compassion. Improving your Self-Esteem helps you to connect to your sense of Self-Worth.

From my experience of working with thousands of people, every person has the capacity for high Self-Esteem, i.e., to have a favorable opinion of themselves. Self-Esteem is not bragging about how great you are; it's more like quietly knowing that you're worth a lot—that you are priceless. It's not about thinking that you are perfect, but knowing that you are worthy of being loved and accepted. Self-Esteem is critical and is a cornerstone of a positive attitude towards living. It is very important because it affects how we think, act and even how we relate to others.

Moving from Thomaston to Prichard introduced me and my family to violence, drugs, gangs, crime, and more. After moving to the inner city, I suffered from low Self-Esteem because of the negative influences in and around my environment. I allowed my childhood peers to cripple me, and I stopped believing in myself. I allowed myself to succumb to the "street life" in order to survive in the inner city. In fear of being rejected or hurt physically and emotionally by my new environment and peers, I had to become a "bad ass" where being bad was the norm. I closed my heart to my real Self; I became what others influenced me to become. All my country-boy goodness was challenged—you would no longer recognize me. My real caring, open and honest Self was being overtaken by an aggressive and tough street kid.

Moving to the City

My older brother Lee loaded all of our possessions on the back of a pick-up truck and moved us into a small house in Prichard, a city with a population of 45,000 people, on the outskirts of Mobile, Alabama. My mother found a job cleaning houses part-time and began establishing herself as the pillar of the community for helping others. She soon became well-known for her famous vanilla-flavored, sugary T-cake biscuits. My alcoholic stepfather worked odds-and-ends jobs as a handyman and occasionally contributed to the family only when my mother fussed about it. My older sisters found odd jobs while my older brothers found construction jobs building bridges to help contribute to our large family's needs. Unfortunately, they soon ventured out into the world, started their own families, and no longer helped to support our family, leaving us to struggle to make ends meet.

When my family moved to Prichard, I was still very young; I was just in the second grade. I went from being a farm boy waking up in the morning to the sounds of nature, running in the fields, climbing hills playing with animals, and catching crawfish in the creek—to the fast pace of city life. Being so young and just a farm boy by nature, I now felt lost and vulnerable in this complex city. People worked outside the community so there were little or no positive role models. Despite my young age, I was trying to find out where I belonged, where I fit in…and my self-esteem suffered for not knowing. It is difficult to have a sense of worth when you grew up feeling that other kids looked down on you for being poor and having family problems. I found myself struggling to excel in school and community. I did not like school in Prichard. I went because it afforded me the opportunity to play sports with my friends and have at least two meals a day—something no longer guaranteed at home.

In the city, kids hung out in groups and didn't work at their daily chores like we did back in Thomaston. These city kids had a pack mentality that drew me in and made me feel like I belonged, but it wasn't a healthy relationship. However, when I joined with them, I did not realize that they would take advantage of my naiveté. The older peers easily swayed and often bullied me into fighting, stealing, shoplifting, etc. I made bad choices because I wanted to belong and be accepted as part of the group which was in reality a gang. I became a juvenile delinquent who had close brushes with the law. I often felt depressed and angry about life and the future. I was in a vicious cycle of low self-worth, underachievement and depression.

Up until my junior high school year, I anxiously awaited my summer school breaks when I could return to Thomaston to visit my relatives and all my animal friends on the farm. I stayed at the home of my beloved sister, Dessie, until she died in 1974, then I started staying with my Uncle Clark and his family. Thomaston remained a place where life was still simple and where people still practiced true Southern Hospitality; they had pride and dignity, they cared about each other and looked out for the children in the community…and fathers were a part of home life. Here, back on the farm, I could escape from the harsh reality of the inner-city life in Prichard where I felt out of place. I was able to renew my worth just by being back in the country sunshine. My mind, body and soul once again connected to a familiar place where I could feel freedom by running in the meadows of purple and yellow flowers or lying under the plum patch and picking black and red berries along barbwire fences. I could run through the rows of fruits and vegetables that we grew ourselves—corn, peas, okra, peanuts, etc. and I could eat watermelon on the front porch all day. This was pure joy.

When I lived in the inner-city, I thought that I had to prove how street-smart I was and believed that I had to be perfect in the eyes of others. I hid my true feelings so that I wouldn't be viewed as weak and so that I could live to play another day. I felt uncomfortable, insecure and did not trust others. My self-esteem was hanging in the balance, and it could have gone either way. My low self-esteem made me see everything negatively. I found myself struggling to be accepted; I felt uncomfortable and misunderstood whenever I was with people—I didn't know how to say the right words or crack a joke to make people laugh. My low self-esteem affected how I related to others and how others related to me. It caused me to under-estimate my abilities and affected my self-determination; I was expected to fail in school and life and so I did. At times, this death sentence caused depression, indecision and inaction. I compromised who I was and lost sight of my true Worth. My Concept of Self had been altered.

Looking back over my country and inner-city lives in Thomaston and Mobile, respectively, I now understand that "I gotta be me." By learning where we come from, we gain insight into understanding who we really are. I am no longer ashamed of who I was because I am now aware of how these two different life styles impacted and shaped my life and helped me to become the person that I am today.

Dr. Abraham Maslow, the well-known psychiatrist and behaviorist, believed that acceptance of Self and others (and all their imperfections) was a key trait of persons who valued themselves regardless of their shortcomings, weaknesses or frailties. These self-actualized people accept their own human nature with all of its discrepancies. They accept themselves in the same unquestioning spirit with which one accepts nature. One does not complain about water because it is wet, about rocks because they are hard or about trees because they are green.[29] You are who you are!

Too often, we discourage and sell ourselves short by looking only at our physical, mental or financial limitations and we attribute these things to our lack of happiness. We tell ourselves that we are too old, too young, too dumb, too sick, too shy, too afraid, too poor, or any other "too."[30] And, yes, we all have limits. But perpetuating them, instead of overcoming them, takes away our Self-Esteem. By retaining these self-limiting thoughts, beliefs and images, we create a negative opinion of ourselves instead of believing that we really are important and valuable.

Self-Esteem affects our outlook on life and those around us. "I gotta be me"—is that okay with you?

Self-Confidence

"You gain strength, courage and confidence by every experience in which you really stop to look fear in the face. You are able to say to yourself, 'I have lived through this horror. I can take the next thing that comes along.' You must do the thing you think you cannot do."

~ Eleanor Roosevelt

Without Self-Confidence you will struggle with Self-Esteem. Work on your Self-Confidence and you will build your Self-Esteem and vice versa. These traits are two sides of the same coin.

The dictionary defines Self-Confidence as freedom from doubt and belief in yourself and your abilities. Confidence is synonymous with trust which is a firm reliance on the integrity, ability or character of a person or thing.

Do you have confidence in who you are and what you do? Do you have confidence in others? Why aren't more people confident in themselves? How do you become more confident?

Self-Confidence is a belief in yourself and what you can do. It is the certainty that you are doing your absolute best. It's a feeling that prevents you from being discouraged and has a positive

---

[29]-Abraham H. Maslow, *Motivation and Personality* (New York: Harper & Row, 1954). Citation: Tom G. Stevens, *You Can Choose To Be Happy*, Chap 5, Part 3, Self-Acceptance, The Keys to Eliminating Guilt and Anger, http://www.csulb.edu/~tstevens/h53accep.htm. Accessed Mar 2011.
[30] Ibid.

effect on your relationships, doubts, fears, and insecurities. Self-Confidence is the difference between feeling unstoppable vs. feeling scared out of your wits.

Confidence is putting trust in yourself. It is an attitude which allows you to have a positive, yet realistic, view of yourself and your situation. It allows you to believe in your ability to achieve any goal you desire. People who believe in themselves take charge of their actions. They act assertively, speak calmly and listen properly. Mastering confidence allows us to implement positive change, to build and sustain positive relationships, behaviors and attitudes, to identify priorities, and to manage time in a way that is consistent with our goals.

Confidence is a state of hopefulness that events will be favorable. This attitude allows us to emphasize our worth, our strengths and to give ourselves credit for everything we attempt to do. While we may feel quite confident in academics or athletics, we may not feel confident in our personal appearance or social relationships. We are able to applaud ourselves for our efforts rather than emphasizing the end results of those efforts.

Confident people are flexible and spontaneous. Having confidence does not mean that individuals think that they will be able to do everything; self-confident people have expectations that are realistic. Even when their expectations are not met, they continue to stay positive.

Confidence starts with our Self. It allows us to accept ourselves as we are and others as we find them. As confident people, we trust our own abilities and believe that, within reason, we will be able to focus on and accomplish what we wish for or plan to do. Confidence gives us the passion and the ability to dream.

"One important key to success is self-confidence."
~ Arthur Ashe (1943-1993)[31]

Confidence is the outward sign of inner certainty. Let positive thoughts dominate your thinking. This may be difficult at first, but force yourself to say: "I am strong," "I like myself," "I am worthy," "I can handle what comes my way." It cannot be done overnight, but when you believe you deserve success, it will come your way.

While directing the Tampa Bay Academy of Hope mentoring programs for at-risk youth,[32] I constantly stressed that anything

---

[31]Arthur Ashe, born in Richmond, Virginia, was a tennis star of the 1960s and '70s and an African-American pioneer: the first black man to win at the U.S. Open and Wimbledon.
[32]I founded The Tampa Bay Academy of Hope in July 1996 as a non-profit corporation. See the section "My Legacy..."

was possible and encouraged hope in the minds and hearts of all who attended and worked there, especially those who felt worthless. As they learned the power of their Human Worth, their lives were transformed and they began to have confidence in themselves. Having them participate in new experiences, sampling a wider variety of life in a positive light, did wonders for their confidence. They were encouraged to try something new and different, such as eating mussels in a restaurant, to give them the confidence to know that they can find satisfaction outside their comfort zone.

Working with the Academy's at-risk youth, I also stressed the importance of setting goals no matter how impossible they may seem at the time. With each goal achieved, no matter how small, anyone can become inspired and gain confidence. Never minimize your active part in those goal-achieving efforts by saying, "Oh, I was just lucky!" With every success, you must congratulate yourself and, in doing so, you will build and reinforce your confidence.

A lack of Self-Confidence may have several different aspects: guilt, anger-turned-inward, unrealistic expectations of perfection, a false sense of humility, fear of change or making mistakes, depression, etc. When we are not confident, we are like babies in a cradle depending on others to always take care of us and give us their approval. We often find ourselves avoiding risks due to the fear of failure, and we generally do not expect to be successful. Without a sense of confidence, we often put ourselves down and tend to discount or ignore compliments paid to us. We may be put into a frantic state to pursue all sorts of material things that don't give our lives value. We make poor judgments and do not feel good about our worth.

If you lack confidence in yourself and are uncertain in your arguments, you will not be able to persuade others. In contrast, being self-confident means being willing to risk the disapproval of others because one trusts in one's own abilities—and rejects the need to conform in order to be accepted.

Surprisingly, lack of Self-Confidence is not necessarily related to lack of ability. Instead, it is often the result of focusing too much on the unrealistic expectations or standards of others, especially parents and society. Parents' attitudes are crucial to children's feelings about themselves, particularly in their early years. When parents provide acceptance, children receive a solid foundation for good feelings about themselves. If one or both parents are excessively critical or demanding, or if they are overprotective and discourage independence, children may believe they are incapable, inadequate or inferior. However, if parents encourage children's self-reliance and accept and love their children when they make mistakes, children will learn to accept themselves and will be on their way to developing Self-Confidence.

Peer influences can be as powerful or more powerful than those of parents or society in shaping feelings about ourselves. While at Southern University in Louisiana, my peers and mentors gave me a sense of confidence in my abilities. I did not believe I was college material, but people believed in me and my potential. College gave me the opportunity to develop my own identity, especially at a time when I was particularly vulnerable to the influence of friends. The positive reinforcement that I received instilled such confidence in me that I trusted myself to "make it" despite my academic limitations. I was able to re-connect to and re-examine my worth.

Athletes all have something in common—they understand winning and losing a game—and, like life, you win some and lose some. Playing sports pushes one's abilities to endure pain and setbacks, face challenges, exercise discipline, and overcome obstacles. It is important to talk yourself into trying things that seem impossible. In sports, success is the only goal—and each success generates more confidence to continue to attempt or perform something even more difficult.

Self-Confidence is contagious. Athletics gave me the vibes that made me feel I had strength and energy. My coaches and teammates established and set the standards for overcoming all odds and winning. Being a part of a sports team significantly boosted my confidence. My teammates inspired me with shouts of "Come on!" and "You can do it." Coaches convinced me that the goals ahead were attainable and within my capabilities. With their encouragement, I found myself constantly attempting to do things slightly more difficult than the last. When I heard their encouraging words, "good job," "excellent," "well done," and "you did your best," it reinforced my Self-Confidence about being a great player. My coaches' confidence-instilling feedback was reinforced by my repeating their messages over and over again in my mind as a form of self-persuasion. I believed that if my teammates could do it, so could I.

Thanks to the support of my coaches and teammates, I was able to stay confident and focus on performing with a winning attitude. Throughout my pre-college and college years, I gained the athletic skills and abilities that prepared me to play in the NFL. Confidence is gained in knowing you are well-prepared and have the skills and ability to do whatever it is you need to do. I was confident in knowing exactly what I needed to do and knew that I would not fail. A lack of Self-Confidence causes missed opportunities, hesitation and a lack of action.

College Football

High school graduation was a remarkable time for me. After discovering that I had a natural talent as an athlete, I graduated in 1982 from Mattie T. Blount High School in Prichard, Alabama, and received a full four-year football scholarship to attend Southern University in Baton Rouge, Louisiana. I was the first in my family to graduate from high school. I knew that the scales of life had tipped in my favor, and I had choices my 8 older brothers and 3 older sisters only dreamed about. The teachers in my past who thought I would not amount to much were proven wrong. I realized that I was walking off the commencement stage and into the real world earning the right to walk proudly onto the grounds of Southern University in Baton Rouge, Louisiana.

I can remember when the universities and colleges started recruiting me to play football. They wanted me, the "Gladiator," to play at their colleges and universities despite the fact that I was struggling to maintain a decent grade point average.

I had no idea what I was going to major in, let alone what courses to take when I got to college. I had no examples in my family to follow—I did not know what to expect on a college campus. I worried a lot and the stress led to a lot of soul-searching about whether or not I could perform and succeed in the college environment. My Concept of Self was being threatened by the challenges of higher education.

Poverty was part of the excess baggage that I had taken with me when I set out for college. My family was not able to give me the finer things of life, but their gifts of pride, dignity and self-respect were priceless in my eyes. Although I grew up in poverty, I was not without pride. When my college coach wanted to alter my scholarship and have me obtain financial assistance through other sources, being a young athlete, I balked at the idea. I was not willing to compromise my integrity by accepting financial aid. I knew I could have gone to college with the aid of federal government grants, but I did not have to because I had earned a four year athletic scholarship. My coach and I quickly reached an impasse. The coach wanted to offer another athlete the scholarship I earned, while securing me through other means, but I stood strong on my principles. I earned that scholarship, and no one was going to take it away without a fight. I was not looking for a hand out; I only needed a hand up.

While in high school, athletes had always been given special privileges but those seemed like child's play on a college campus. When I landed on the campus of Southern University, the door to a whole new world opened, and I was invited inside. Because I was a football player, many things that others had to work for were given to me on a silver platter. For the first time in my life, the world seemed at my disposal, and I was enjoying it immensely. The outside world saw me as a young man who beat the luck of the draw and landed on easy street. I saw a young man who had been given a hand up, but who had to work hard every day to keep it.

I promised myself that failure was not an option and football was my one-way ticket out of despair. I was not just making it for me; I was making it for all my family members who fell victim to violence and died too young. I was making it for my mother who struggled her entire life and seemed to be spinning her wheels in the same spot, never advancing. I was making it for all of the children in my old neighborhood, and I was making it for the man I was destined to become.

The battle with my coach ended because I would not relinquish my scholarship, and the coach would not budge on his position. We got into a heated discussion, and he fired me from the team. My response was, "You can't fire me...I quit!" Even though I was recognized by the all-conference team at the end of the season as an outstanding player, I packed my bags at the end of my sophomore year and returned to Prichard.

The return home was the perfect prescription for me; it allowed me the opportunity to see that Prichard was no place for a young man with dreams. It harbored all of the things I had left behind. At college, I had been living in a very sheltered world where the coaches protected me from reality and blocked all of the harmful elements of the real world. I longed for that sheltered atmosphere.

After a full semester had passed, I wanted to return to school. I swallowed my pride and lived off-campus for the Fall semester in order to accomplish my long-term goals. I still had my childhood passion and dream to become a professional football player. I was determined to get back on the team to fulfill this dream. During the Spring semester, I reconciled with the coach and returned to the football field for my senior year. Even after sitting out my junior year, I became a starter for the team. The world was watching me, and it was my job to excel and set an example. My ears exploded with the sounds of thousands of fans screaming for me to go forth and do well. I was a leader and able to encourage others through my own actions. I had become to others what my coaches had been to me. It was now my turn to serve as an inspiration. It was my turn to stand as an example to a little child equipped only with his dreams and a desire to escape the throes of poverty.

I learned that I had a sense of worth and that the only limitations I faced were those that were self-imposed. I found in myself a passion that burned like a fire that could not be extinguished. I learned how to channel that passion and share it with others as an author and motivational speaker. I learned how to teach others to find their strengths and build upon them, bringing out the best in themselves. Today, I have mastered the art of being a leader who is willing to share his passion to make the world a better place for everyone. I am now the person who is giving the hand up, instead of a hand out.

Reflecting back on my love and passion for athletics, I can see why I still have a burning desire to work hard and perform at a superior level. The hard work, the positive mental attitude and teamwork of athletics all helped me to develop the positive strength and determination to overcome and transcend what I thought I couldn't do. Athletics gave me the discipline and inner-strength to withstand hard blows to both the physical body and the emotional mind.

Throughout my life, playing football, track and field, basketball, and even a little baseball appear to have given me the assurance that my life had meaning, purpose and value; they brought out the best in me. I may not have been the smartest kid, may not have made all good grades or belonged to a rich family, but I believed in my abilities, skills and talents and was always willing to work hard. My Self-Confidence complements my Worth and comes from a perspective of having overcome adversity, "put-downs" and setbacks.

My Self-Confidence continues to allow me to attempt to accomplish things that I never would have dreamed of. In 1991, I established YouthBuild, USA in Tampa, Florida. In 1996, I founded the Tampa Bay Academy of Hope, an organization that helps at-risk youth, also in Tampa. I created and published the largest black business directory in all of Tampa. Confidence allowed me to turn lemons into lemonade.

Throughout my athletic life, the confidence I gained gave me the self-control, the will power and strength to give myself permission to rely on the power of my Human Worth. Today, whenever I practice sports, it enables me to feel confident because I can still hear the voices of my coaches and teammates encouraging me to succeed. This Self-Confidence continues to allow me to overcome my past and present circumstances and to give me the strength to overcome my anxieties, fears and the negative influences that impact my life.

Self-Confidence is our self-assuredness in our personal judgment, ability, power, etc. It is an internal determination or judgment of how sure you are of your skill and ability to succeed in a task. There are brilliant talents and capabilities that lie dormant and unused inside each of us. Self-Confidence allows us to seek out and use those skills and enhance our Human Worth.

By believing in ourselves, there is no limit to what we can accomplish. It's time for a change. Let's eliminate our negative thinking, develop a sense of Self-Confidence and overcome any fear of failure. With confidence, we can conquer the difficult and impossible tasks in our lives. With confidence, we can muster the courage to change our destinies. Successful people have Self-Confidence—it's vital that you work on yours! Ask yourself, "Can I do it?" and the answer should be, "Yes, I can!"

Self-Love

"When we make the decision to love ourselves unconditionally, we accept ourselves unconditionally. We are at one with ourselves."
~ John Bradshaw, writer[33]

What is Love? This is one of the most difficult questions for all mankind. Love has been defined as a strong, positive emotion of regard and affection; having a great affection or liking for; to get pleasure from. It usually refers to tendencies in caring for another person. The perception of love presented to us in movies, songs and talk-shows is, too often, not real or genuine which gives us a false sense of what real love is. Love is a basic emotion that we all feel and is important to what gives our lives meaning and purpose. Sadly, some forget that human beings are created out of love and need it without strings attached. Before we can continue to build on the foundation that identifies who we are, we must evaluate our opinion of who we think we are.

Self-Love is loving one's self without judgment and being happy with who you are despite your flaws. We don't have to follow trends or paths others have laid out for us. True Self-Love does not need the validation of others. It is being in love with one's self in a humble way.

The song title and 1993 movie, "What's Love Got To Do With It?"[34] depicts the gritty, intimate and poignant true life story of R&B/pop singer Tina Turner and documents her efforts to break away from her abusive husband. Her husband constantly called her derogatory names and physically abused her. Tina Turner allowed him to control her because she lacked unconditional love of herself. She allowed her self-image to be distorted by his damaging opinions of her. She lost sight of her Human Worth!

We must not depend on someone else to make us feel loved. But sometimes loving ourselves can be difficult. How can we love

---

[33]John Bradshaw, *Healing the Shame That Binds You* (Deerfield Park, FL: Publisher Health Communication, Inc., 2005), p 225.
[34] Dir. Brian Gibson, Perf. Angela Bassett, Laurence Fishburne, Touchstone Production Co.

ourselves when other people keep telling us that we are "selfish" or "stupid?" Our Self-Worth can be so badly damaged that we will blame ourselves and others for our perceived inadequacies. After many, many years of marriage, Tina Turner arrived at the point where, rather than resenting her ex-husband for the pain he inflicted upon her, she forgave him. The people who hurt us are often put in our path to teach us forgiveness.

While it is important to have compassion and love for others, how can we respect and love others if we don't respect and love ourselves? When we embrace loving ourselves, we come to the realization that we no longer need to depend on others to love us. To truly understand our worth is to realize that we don't need the love or approval of others to be who we are destined to be.

To love ourselves is to give ourselves permission to grow, mature and evolve. To love ourselves is accepting who we are at face value while striving to improve our inner selves which reinforces and compliments our worth. To love ourselves is to realize that physical appearance does not dictate who we are or limit who we can become. To love ourselves is just as important as breathing the air that gives you life.

Do you expect someone else to make you feel safe and loved, wanted and desired? Having true unconditional love for yourself means finding the true you. When was the last time you really focused on finding out who YOU really are? You must master the art of Self-Love before you can realize your true worth.

What is "unconditional" love? Unconditional love is a term that means to love someone regardless of their actions or beliefs. It is a concept comparable to true love, a term which is more frequently used to describe love between lovers. Unconditional love is frequently used to describe love between family members, comrades-in-arms, etc. or with your pets who love you no matter what you look like or who you are.

We must learn to love ourselves unconditionally and understand that happiness can come from Self-Love. Loving yourself unconditionally allows you to connect to your human-worth despite any physical, emotional, mental or spiritual handicaps. It is no exaggeration to say that our emotional need for unconditional Self-Love is just as great as our physical need for air, water and food. We think about it, hope for it, fantasize about it, go to great lengths to achieve it, and feel that our lives are incomplete without it. Unconditional or true Self-Love is the only kind of love that can make us whole and give us the true happiness we all want. It is unconditional Self-Love that we all seek and somehow we intuitively realize that anything else isn't really love at all—it's an imitation of the real thing. Self-Love enables you to discover the real value in yourself. Self-Love encourages us to truly be ourselves.

My misconceptions about unconditional love began in early childhood. While growing up, my parents, teachers, peers, and others gave praise, love and affection if and only if I attended church, was well dressed, quiet, obedient, or well-behaved; they seldom gave it just because I needed it. My family and friends smiled at me and spoke in kind and gentle tones. But when I wasn't a good little boy and behaved badly, the love instantly disappeared. We all want to feel loved. Love is the common denominator that connects us to our worth. Loving ourselves without judgment is being happy with who we are now.

Now that I'm older and have embraced my Human Worth I know that the love I received was conditional and that I was "buying" love from the people around me with my words, appearances and behavior. People believe that they can buy unconditional love and feel fulfilled. However, they pay a price when they attempt to buy love by gaining the approval and respect of others; this only provides a false sense of feeling loved. We must love ourselves regardless of others' actions or beliefs. How long are we willing to pay the cost for a false sense of feeling loved? We must learn to love ourselves with deep and enduring emotion. When, through conscious effort, we learn to love ourselves unconditionally, we will be willing and able to love others unconditionally as well. Be aware that it is absolutely impossible to unconditionally love yourself if you harbor bitterness, anger, guilt or any feelings that limit your ability to love others. We will not be able to rid ourselves of our own anger unless we can truly accept or forgive others. We will not have inner harmony if we accept imperfections in ourselves and do not accept them in others; that inconsistency creates disharmony.

With unconditional love there are no limitations, conditions or reservations put on the love that we want to fill our lives with. We must love ourselves during our good and bad times. Loving ourselves validates and compliments our true worth.

I want to address one myth I became aware of while growing up as a Christian. I kept hearing that we are *not* capable of unconditional love. According to *my* Bible, we were born with unconditional love. Genesis 1:27: *"So God created man in his own image, in the image of God created he him; male and female created he them. God is the Alpha and the Omega. The beginning and the end of unconditional love."*

God is the essence of unconditional love. God *is* unconditional love. I believe that when God created us in His image He endowed us with the spirit of unconditional love. When we display unconditional love we are, in effect, in His Spirit and we are blessed. To love unconditionally means our motives are pure.

When I wrote and self-published a book entitled "James M. Evans Meeting Himself For The Very First Time"[35] it helped me to understand myself. It helped me to understand my worth and love myself unconditionally. Before this self-reflection, I always had to achieve something more before I could be happy. I never had enough success to prove that I was "OK" as a human being. Consequently, I never believed that anyone—including my wife— could really love me, but once you genuinely demonstrate that you love yourself, you will find that others will love you just for being you.

The world owes you nothing. You were born deserving love, so was everyone else. My goal everyday is to live a life with unconditional Self-Love and compassion for others so that I can fulfill my dreams and leave the world a better place. We are each on our own journey to connect to our worth and realize and maximize our potential. Love is the basis for everything you are and wish to be. When we learn to love ourselves for who we are or, at least, accept every part of ourselves, we can connect to our worth and gain happiness.

Every morning upon awakening you should look in the mirror and say, "I love myself!" Every morning you should make the conscious effort to love yourself unconditionally. Love yourself and look within to find the strength to make the choices that will provide the greatest fulfillment in your life. This is not a selfish act! It is merely one of many choices you have. You have the power to choose the directions you feel are best for yourself. YOU have to take the initiative and DO this!

Self-Determination

"If you are determined, nothing is impossible." ~ Anonymous

Self-Determination is one's freely expressed will exercised by one's personal control to determine one's visions and dreams. It means controlling your own fate or course of action without external compulsion. Self-Determination compels you to make the most out of life and maximize your potential. When you are at your

---

[35] James M. Evans, *The Autobiography of James M. Evans: Meeting Himself for the Very First Time.* (Tampa, FL: Eagle Quest Group, 2005).

53

highest point of worth, it is your natural tendency to perform and lead a balanced, purpose-driven life.

There is a story about a little girl who told her teacher that some day she wanted to be successful. The teacher grabbed her by her ankles and dunked her head first into a barrel of water standing nearby. While under the water, the little girl kicked and struggled for what it was worth. After a minute or so, the teacher lifted the little girl out of the barrel of water and stood her upright. As the little girl was breathing very hard, the teacher asked the little girl, "When you were underwater what did you want more than anything else in life?" The little girl replied, "I wanted air." The teacher responded by saying, "When you want success as much as you wanted that air, you will have it." The moral of the story is that to be successful you have to be as determined as much as you want to live.

Self-Determination differs from person to person according to what each individual desires to create a satisfying and personally meaningful life. Self-determined individuals decide where they will live and with whom; what commitments they will make to achieve their dreams; which vocational or educational opportunities they wish to engage in...or...*not* doing any of these things.

"And so I tell you, keep on asking, and you will receive what you ask for. Keep on seeking, and you will find. Keep on knocking, and the door will be opened to you. For everyone who asks, receives. Everyone who seeks, finds. And to everyone who knocks, the door will be opened."
(Luke 11:9-10)

Choice is central to Self-Determination. Many times people have very limited choices. They often cannot choose very important aspects of their lives, such as where they live or with whom. For instance, individuals may be able to choose who their roommate will be, but not whether or not they will have one. At other times, selections are only somewhat limited—how they will spend their time, money or even what they eat. True choice is being able to pick from the same wide variety of lifestyles, goals and individual preferences most people enjoy.

Support is a keystone to making Self-Determination work. Most people have some type of support network in their lives that they turn to when they must make an important decision or take a step forward in their lives. The self-determined individual selects and invites each member of his or her circle of support. They can be family members, friends or people from the community--anyone that the person desires. Most importantly, they are people with whom the individual has or wishes to build a trusting relationship.

While most people are supported in the decision-making process, Self-Determination gives *you* the final say and ownership of your life. Ownership implies more than just decision-making; it means that you are the final and total authority—the boss. Ownership means you have control over your life and that you accept the risk and responsibility for your actions and decisions.

To actively develop your Self-Determination, view yourself as *not* having limitations that prevent you from participating fully in life. Picture yourself as a valuable human being who has many talents, strengths and abilities to contribute to society. See yourself as an individual with rights and entitlements and make the right choices to take individual control of your life.

"Self-Determination is what life is all about. Without it, you might be alive, but you wouldn't be living–you would just be existing"[36]

My life did not always have a clear direction. Time and time again, I failed to focus on what was truly worthwhile. I wasted time and energy on meaningless activities that did not accomplish anything for me in the long run. This was largely due to my not having goals or a real purpose in life. Throughout my teenage years, I was very self-critical and devalued my worth thus undermining any Self-Determination I might have had...I was a mere shadow of whom I could have been. I lacked the support needed for making important decisions or taking a step forward in my life. I did not have ownership of my life, nor did I have the final and total authority to make decisions.

The Shaping of a Teenager

By all accounts, I was a product of what has become known as a "dysfunctional family." While my family may have been "dysfunctional," it was the only one I knew anything about. During my formative teenage years, we moved five times. I was an 8 year old country boy when we first moved to Prichard. It did not help matters that we had moved to a community where wealth was absent, but drugs and alcohol were prevalent. As a result, I began drinking and experimenting with drugs. I was confronted with neighborhood bullies and gangs. I witnessed things that a young child should never see.

By the time I was a teenager, I suddenly realized that I was on my own. I could leave my house, and no one kept track of where I was or what I was doing. During the summer, when I was not home in the country, I spent much of my time at the

---

[36] M. Kennedy, "Self-Determination and Trust: My Experiences and Thoughts," In Sands & Wehmeyer, eds., *Self-Determination Across the Life Span* (Baltimore, MD: Paul H. Brookes, 1996), p 48.

community park and recreation center directly behind my house. A middle-aged woman named Ms. Lott operated it, and many of the other neighborhood children sought refuge there as well. We were provided a free lunch and our days were filled with many activities, such as swimming, arts and crafts, and baseball. I spent many hours swimming during the long, hot summers, but the bullies found me no matter where I was. On a regular basis, I was faced with these situations that I could not walk away from; I had to decide either to fight and defend myself or resist the anger and become the prey. I was forced to either allow myself to become a victim or find a way to pull myself up from the valley of despair. To me, it was a no-brainer—I had to fight to protect myself, and many times these fights led to school expulsions.

While in Prichard Middle School, sports became my game changer—and saved my sense of worth. During these summers, I spent less time in the country with my older sister and uncle and began to take a major interest in sports. My first encounter with athletics was when I tried out as a pitcher for the baseball team. I did not think I was any good in the sport, so I gave up quickly. But then I discovered basketball, football, and track and field. When I started playing football and track and field, a lot of good things happened. Suddenly, I became interested in school. Coaches praised me for my hard work and showed confidence in me. My increased success in track and field and little league football increased my confidence with people. I got into less trouble. I decided to change my life. I studied harder, but I still struggled to maintain passing grades. I had found my passion—I wanted to become a successful professional football player.

James - high school junior year

By the time I reached high school, I was a well-behaved student and didn't cause much trouble. I had all but abandoned basketball and now concentrated more fully on football. This would be my ticket out of poverty.

Who knows which road in my life I would have taken if it had not been for Coach George Walker and Coach Joe Collins. These two men, one black and one white, respectively, became sources of inspiration for the young men who wanted to rise above their humble surroundings. They protected the students, sometimes even from themselves, and helped me to realize my potential. They were not just interested in the potential athlete; they were concerned about the total person.

I put my heart into athletics and began running track and playing football. I soon discovered that with less idle time, there were fewer opportunities to get into *trouble. The neighborhood still had its share of trouble for anyone looking for it, but I set my eyes on a higher prize and knew that getting caught up in gang fights or other distractions was not the life for me. I filled my days with studying in order to keep my grades up and with practicing after-school. I also found a job in the neighborhood working for a woman who owned rental property. If someone had asked me then about my future, I would have told them that nothing is free, but everything is available if you want it badly enough and are willing to work hard enough for it.*

We are all faced with choices and options in our daily lives, and Self-Determination supports our natural or inner tendency to behave in effective and healthy ways. Self-Determination expands those opportunities by allowing and encouraging us to explore the possibilities that are present in ourselves—our abilities to take risks, to make mistakes and to grow from them.

Johnny Mercer, an American lyricist, songwriter and singer from Savannah, Georgia, said it best, "you've got to eliminate the negative, accentuate the positive, latch on to the affirmative, and don't mess with Mr. In-between."[37] When I was recruited by the NFL as a running back, I was determined to make it by never giving up and never giving in. I was determined to achieve what I had always dreamed about as a kid. The NFL was a place where I had to prove my worth and lay claim to my future. I was driven to do whatever it took to avoid going home with my tail tucked between my legs.

"Believe you can and you're half way there."
~ Theodore Roosevelt, former U.S. president

My Stint in the NFL

It was my rural country attitude and positive behavior along with my inner-city toughness that paid off and played a major role in getting me into college and the National Football League. I had total confidence that I could become a professional football player. Football in the inner city carried a prestige and was a way out of crime and poverty for at-risk-youth. I accomplished what almost every little, inner-city boy fantasizes and dreams about—playing professional football.

I felt like Superman. I was on a mission. I had been given a glimpse of what the future could hold for me and giving up was never an option. I was not so consumed with making it that I was blind to reality. I remember all too clearly when I was kicked off the team at the end of my sophomore year because my coach and I had

---

[37] Lyrics from his song, "Accentuate the Positive," 1945, Capital-EMI record label.

a major disagreement. Despite this setback, I came back in my junior year and continued to train with all of my might to fulfill my boyhood dream. I swallowed my pride and asked the coach to allow me to play again. He consented, and I became the only senior to be drafted by an NFL team. This victory was even sweeter in that I was drafted despite the fact that I had not played my junior year. I beat all the odds.

The Kansas City Chiefs chose me in the 10th round as a running back (#41) and that day solidified my future. Once a wide-eyed country boy, I was leaving college in Baton Rouge, Louisiana, as a drafted professional athlete. My chances of making the team were slim—I was a long-shot. I now found myself in Kansas City, Missouri, attending the football camps with the chosen elite. The NFL life now exposed me to things I had only read about in books and magazines or seen on television. In the NFL, I had many "first" experiences, such as riding on a luxury private airplane, living in luxurious hotels and meeting people from all walks of life and from all over the world. It was an experience without a price tag. All players shared the same passion and dream - to play in the NFL.

James on the Kansas City Chiefs 1987

I was naïve to the ways of the world; I thought that I had been chosen because I was a good specimen. I took to the field with everything in me. I played like a man possessed and never gave any thought to not being chosen when the rounds of cuts were made. I did not know it at the time, but it was not the intention of the coaches to keep me on the team. I was chosen to push the other three running backs to do better and make them perform to their maximum. Since I was uninformed of this, I remained a driven and passionate player who refused to be stopped. I became a force to be reckoned with on the practice field. Not only could I catch the ball exceptionally well and break the long yard runs, but I was the best blocking back on the team. In the final analysis, the coaches suddenly found themselves in unfamiliar territory. They had to admit that I, the underdog, had proven myself—they had to make me the third-down running back despite my originally being picked in the 10th round.

The coaches also were forced to look at three other rookie running backs trying out for the team. They were number 35, Christian Okoye of Azusa Pacific (chosen in the second round), number 26, Paul Palmer of Temple (a first-round pick) and number 46, Michael Clemmons of William and Mary (chosen in the 8th round). They too made the cut, and we became known as the Four Horsemen. No other team in NFL history had ever kept four running back draft picks on their roster. My life was taking shape and things were going in the right direction for me.

When I became a professional football player, I was in the less than 1% of the "high earners" that were "guaranteed" to make it in professional sports. I was sold the bill of goods that sports were what I needed to value—that being a professional athlete constituted my real worth—and I foolishly perceived it as my real Self. Being a "gladiator" gave me a deep sense of accomplishment, success and a self-confidence that boosted my self-esteem tremendously; I was energized, motivated, and passionate about "the game." Little did I realize how confused I was about the real me. It's very important that we understand that our Concept of Self is continuously changing with time and that we may go through turbulent periods of identity crisis and reassessment.

I had spent a major part of my life yearning to become a professional athlete. However, just as I was realizing my dream of being a professional football player, the NFL went on strike, and the owners brought in replacement players. That was the beginning of the end of my professional NFL career as an athlete which lasted only one full season. I only played for the first three games before the strike started, and shortly thereafter, I was released from the Kansas City Chiefs. The Tampa Bay Buccaneers quickly picked up my contract for the remainder of the 1987 season, but released me at the start of the next season after which time my agent secured me a tryout with the San Diego Chargers. But playing ball no longer had the attraction it once did for me, and I realized it was time to walk away. Being married and wanting to stay and settle down in Tampa, Florida, I decided to let go of my childhood hopes and dreams and let my short stint with the NFL end. My vision had changed and being a professional athlete simply was not as important to me as it once was.

I now know that my potential was not on the football field. I needed to sort out my direction and create a plan to make something happen. I held a series of jobs until I found my niche with YouthBuild USA, a not-for-profit organization that gives young adults a second chance by offering them careers in construction. What I learned from this experience became the stepping stone for me to establish the Tampa Bay Academy of Hope, Inc. My new calling was in service to others. I just did not know how I was going to succeed.

It suddenly became clear to me that I still possessed that determination and ambition that I had applied to football. I simply began to channel it in a new direction. If I failed, it was because I did something wrong, but if I succeeded, it was because I did something right. I realized that I would never know if I never tried. I simply trusted in God and had faith and He's been guiding me ever since.

Athletics gave me the discipline that later brought me closer to my real Self. Football was the catalyst that taught me to focus and concentrate—to be "in the zone." The zone is the place where you have to relax your mind, body and soul in order to master the art of playing football. It taught me to quiet the mind of stress, worry, fears, doubt, and negative thoughts. This gave me the inner strength to open up an inner door to my real Self. It brought me closer to making the connection to my self-worth. I started to communicate with others heart-to-heart and with ease. I began to trust and love hard. I was meeting my Self for the very first time.

"A small body of determined spirits fired by an unquenchable faith in their mission can alter the course of history." ~ Mahatma Gandhi

Knowing who we are and knowing who we can become serve as the motivation for our self-determined behaviors and actions.

The Driving Force Within

I cannot pinpoint the exact moment when the idea to help others came to me. But in 1987, while I was a Tampa Bay Buccaneer, I gave a speech, "The ABC's of Motivation" to inspire young people about the importance of their Human Worth. That presentation was the beginning of my desire to motivate others. I learned from that experience how impressionable our young people are and how they yearned for guidance and counseling. Their troubles and struggles reminded me of my own past. When those painful memories returned, they were not specters to haunt me for I no longer feared my past because I had accepted and embraced it. I began to use my past as a tool to help others. It became my mission to shape the hearts and minds of the younger generation.

I had accomplished much in my life. I had beaten the odds and succeeded when everyone thought I would fail. I silenced all of those who felt that I wouldn't amount to much. I had proven them wrong; I attended college and was drafted by the Kansas City Chiefs professional football team. That was a success in itself because many thought I would never make it out of high school. With this success, I should have been content.

During my college life, I was exposed to a new world that I never knew existed. I had been given the magic formula to break free from my environment and make things happen for me. Yet, there was something buried deep inside of me that

would not let my past die. As painful as it was at times, I forced myself to revisit my past. I suddenly realized that I could never be truly free unless I accepted my past and viewed it in the proper perspective. I dissected it, examined each piece of it, and learned how to use it to help others.

Many parts of my past have become teachable moments for others to learn from. I looked at the cycle of poverty from all angles and realized that the cycle could be broken with the right tools. I believed that if poverty, the mother of crime and underachievement, was removed from the equation, then a glimmer of hope would take its place. That hope would breed a sense of belonging and a desire to accomplish. I realized that there were hundreds of teenagers in my community whose present was my past. I knew that I had to reach them because the world had turned its back on them.

I have a genuine, constant and burning passion to serve others. It is a feeling deeply rooted in my soul. I find myself consciously caring for others and wanting to listen to their issues and concerns. In doing so, I am inspired to motivate and make other people's concerns one of my highest priorities.

I knew that I had a weapon in my arsenal to get the job done—one of my talents was the gift of persuasion. I was not afraid to speak before people and express my opinions. I utilized my talent as a speaker to get the attention of those who were in a position to help me make a difference in the lives of disadvantaged youth. I didn't yet consider myself a leader but constantly found myself being placed in that role. It became a newly found revelation that it seemed to be a natural fit for me; I wanted to know more about it.

I suddenly realized that education was the missing element in the lives of the people that I desired to help. But I knew I could not accomplish anything without the support and help of the community.

The doubters and naysayers told me I was attempting the impossible. It became my mission to teach them a lesson with the message that nothing was unattainable. I was a living example of that. I realized, based on my own life, that the impossible just takes longer. I decided to start an organization[38] and struggled to raise monies for it each and every day—in every way that I could. Failure was not an option. With a strong sense of self-worth and self-determination, my hopes and vision became a reality. With each incoming dollar I could see myself grabbing one child by the arm and pulling him or her from the dark abyss of hopelessness.

Self-Determination allows us to see our hopes come true, our dreams fulfilled and our visions made a reality.

---

[38] In 1996 I founded the non-profit Tampa Bay Academy of Hope, Inc.

Self-Respect

Self-Respect is a popular self-help topic and seems to be the medication prescribed for those who have low Self-Esteem. Respect is more than politeness and paying lip service. Many top psychologists argue that Self-Respect is vital for us to flourish and lead a satisfying, meaningful life. In the late 1960's, Abraham Maslow developed a theory of human needs. He stated that when our needs for a high level of Self-Respect and respect from others are satisfied we can then feel self-confident and valuable. When these needs are not met, we are frustrated, feel inferior, weak, helpless, and worthless. Without Self-Respect we are condemned to be restricted and cutoff from possibilities for self-realization, self-fulfillment and happiness.[39]

Self-Respect is defined as a feeling, attitude or trait regarding one's self-honor. It is acknowledging that we have value as a person, recognizing our strengths and abilities and holding ourselves in high esteem. It's admiration or courteous regard for yourself coupled with a concern for one's reputation.

Those who lack Self-Respect rob themselves of dignity which is a struggle to regain once you've lost it. Some people feel cheated out of it, and everyone wants it even to the point that they will kill for it. For many, enduring criticism and insults from family, friends or others, for whatever reason, diminishes our feelings of Self-Respect. When individuals suffer such attacks or let-downs and do not get the admiration they feel they should have and deserve, this will, in turn, often result in that individual showing disrespect towards others.

To overcome this negativity in our lives, it's important to be open-minded and consider the source of the insult and the possible reasons why others are doing what they do. When we acknowledge that the onslaught on our dignity is external (outside of our true Self) and that internally (in our mind, heart and soul) we possess Human Worth, then and only then will we be able to feel the fullness of the respect that we deserve.

[39] Abraham H. Maslow, *A Theory of Human Motivation*, originally published in *Psychological Review* 50 (1943): 381. Citation: Christoper D. Green, *The Esteem Needs*, Classics in the History of Psychology, http://psychclassics.yorku.ca/Maslow/motivation.htm. Accessed Aug 2011.

Self-Dignity

Self-Dignity co-exists with at least three parts of our Concept of Self: Self-Love, Self-Esteem and Self-Confidence. When we have all three traits, our personal value is enhanced, and we feel good about ourselves. Self-Dignity allows us to love ourselves, hold ourselves in high esteem and act with confidence. Self-Dignity is one's personal status of self-importance reflected in one's behaviors and attitudes expressed by the way one talks and even the tone of one's voice. Self-Dignity helps us to maintain a sense of Self-Esteem, Self-control and Self-direction.

I believe Self-Dignity, like our Human Worth, is bestowed upon us at birth. But Self-Dignity is also influenced internally and externally by our sense of Human Worth—how important we feel we are to others and by our external environment and social ties, respectively. These influences validate our sense of dignity—either reinforcing or weakening our feelings of Self-Esteem and confidence. Many of my life experiences should have been enough to rob me of my Self-Dignity, but they didn't. My Self-Dignity somehow survived the negative circumstances of being labeled a dysfunctional learner, living in poverty, not knowing my real father, participating in gangs and violence, using drugs and alcohol, and being abused and hurt emotionally. These combined experiences could have changed my life for the worse, and I could have missed the opportunity for a quality life. Instead, these challenges allowed me to learn a great deal about myself and my family.

Growing up in the country played an important role in how I learned about dignity. Country life in Thomaston, Alabama, imparted to me a sense of honor in the way I should treat others and myself. Because my mother had her own sense of dignity, it was reflected in how she treated others. I often witnessed how she made sacrifices to help others. She fed the hungry, clothed the naked and provided shelter to the homeless –even while taking care of her own large family. She treated everyone with whom she came in contact with a sincere sense of respect and love. Watching my mother treat people with such dignity in a sincere and natural way showed me that everyone was deserving of it. Her actions taught me to show dignity and respect to others even though it would mean that we would often do without enough food. Her dignity, Self-Esteem and confidence instilled it in others. She instilled it in me and, to this day, I follow in her very large footsteps.

Self-Pride

"All anyone asks for is a chance to work with pride."
~ W. Edwards Deming

St. Augustine stated that pride is the "the love of one's own excellence." Self-Pride is the opposite of humility. Self-Pride is sometimes viewed as excessive or as a vice and sometimes viewed as proper or as a virtue. While philosophers like Aristotle and George Bernard Shaw consider pride a profound virtue, most world religions consider it a sin. Some theologians believe that pride is sinful worship of yourself.

Self-Pride is an important link between our Self and our Human Worth. Self-Pride is a self-evaluation or judgment of our personal character or ego. It's a feeling of being proud of who one is—that one is a good person, but not to the point of arrogance or narcissism. It occurs when we have successfully accomplished something and bask in our own glory or achievement. It is a product of praise or criticism from others, but, more importantly, it is also an independent self-reflection on our interactions with and reactions to our own behaviors as they relate to our internal standards or rules.[40] We are proud of ourselves when we fulfill a lifelong goal or can proclaim that we are a good mother, father, leader, or employee. Self-Pride allows us to connect to our sense of worth in a positive manner.

Self-Pride may sometimes give other people a false impression of ourselves. When we feel embarrassment, guilt or shame, we may hide our true selves from other people so that they do not reject us or think badly of us. This deception or hiding of our perceived inadequacies is a reflection of our lack of Self-Worth. We don't' tell the unblemished truth because we are "too proud" and don't want to take responsibility for our shortcomings. This impacts our Concept of Self in a negative manner.

Living in the inner-city of Prichard, Alabama, took its toll on my family's country values including Self-Pride and revealed how vulnerable our Concepts of Self were. In the inner city, kids were arrogant, conceited and disrespectful to authority. This prevalent influence on my family would cause us much sadness and sorrow.

---

[40]Nathaniel Branden discusses the importance of self-reflection in *Honoring the Self: Self-Esteem and Personal Transformation* (New York: Bantam Books, 1984).

My family's rural attitudes, behaviors and ways of thinking did not fit in to this new environment—it would get the best of us, and we would lose sight of our Human Worth.

We were just country folks who worked proudly on the farm picking cotton, rolling hay, posting barbwire fences, and working crops in the fields of nearby landowners. After a hard week of work, we hunted and fished. But all that became like a distant memory; inner-city life tugged at our cores and changed us. We were faced with drugs, alcohol, violence, and struggles for material things. The aggression of bullies made me so angry and fearful that this spilled over into disrespect to my elders and family members who had always greeted me with a smile, praise, laughter, and maybe even with a kiss. I knew my behavior and attitude towards them was wrong. They taught me good values, but the pain and hurt of growing up in the city caused me to lose any pride in myself, and I lost sight of my worth.

Attitude

"The greatest discovery of my generation is that a human being can alter his life by altering his attitudes of minds."
~ William James (1842-1910), American philosopher/psychologist

Charles Swindoll, noted speaker, biblical scholar and author of many religious and self-help books, stated: "The longer I live, the more I realize *the impact of attitude on my Human Worth. Attitude, to me, is more important than facts. It is more important than the past, education, money, circumstances, failures, successes, what other people think or say or do...Attitude will make or break a company, a church, a home. The remarkable thing is that we all have a choice...regarding the attitude we will embrace for that day. We cannot change our past. We cannot change the fact that people will act in a certain way. We cannot change the inevitable. The only thing we can do is play on the string we have, and that is our attitude. I am convinced that life is 10% of what happens to me, and 90% of how I react to it."*[41]

Our attitude is all about the way we think, act and feel about a person, place or thing. It controls the inner peace that we seek. Attitude plays a key role in how we relate and respond to our environment, situations and other people. It is crucial in determining our successes and failures.

---

[41]Cited at http://thinkexist.com/quotes/charles_r._swindoll/. Accessed Nov 2010.

When we want to better ourselves, we should start with our attitude. Attitude and confidence in ourselves make a difference in our pursuit of our goals and dreams. Attitude is not the result of success, but success is the result of a good attitude—thinking, talking, acting, and conducting yourself as the person *you wish to become.*

"Nothing can stop the man with the right mental attitude from achieving his goal; nothing on earth can help the man with the wrong mental attitude."
~ Thomas Jefferson

When we become aware of and believe in the God-given worth within ourselves, we will automatically inherit an attitude which is perhaps our most powerful weapon against defeat. If only we believe, we can become. The Spirit of God guides us as we master a positive attitude which restores our worth and, subsequently, helps determine our successes. In all of our affairs, it is important to think, talk, act, and conduct ourselves in such a way that we reflect our great worth. If we believe that we can only become moderately successful, then we limit our potential. If we keep an open mind and a positive attitude, then there are no limits to what we can accomplish.

"It is very important to generate a good attitude, a good heart, as much as possible. From this, happiness in both the short term and the long term for both yourself and others will come." ~ Dalai Lama

Oftentimes, when we don't feel very good about our worth, we will also have poor attitudes towards others. We will wait for the world to change towards us before we consider changing our own behavior. The right attitude in any given situation is going to determine how far we go in life—there is no halfway point or compromise. Our attitude is like being on trial. The final verdict as to what happens to our attitude will be up to us. We're the judge, the jury and the attorney for both the defense and the prosecutor. We control our mind and shape our destiny.

How do you feel about yourself? What kind of attitude do you have? Do you have a negative or a positive attitude?

The following story was sent to me by one of my former TBAH students: *A young officer in the Army discovered that he had no coin change when he wanted to buy a soft drink from a vending machine. He flagged down a passing private and asked him, "Do you have change for a dollar?" The private said cheerfully, "I think so. Let me take a look." The officer drew himself up stiffly and said,*

"Soldier, that is no way to address a superior. We will start all over again. Do you have change for a dollar?" The private came to stiff attention, saluted smartly and said, "No, sir!"

Now that's a positive attitude!! Each of us can command some authority no matter what. There are or will be those we guide, supervise, rear, mentor, or lead. Some of us will be effective and others will feel as if we're running a cemetery—with people under us, but nobody listening.

It has often been said, "nothing is impossible; the impossible just takes a little longer." This is not to say that we won't encounter obstacles and challenges, but our attitude will determine the level of success we can reach even before we initiate a project. Once you understand your worth, you must be persistent. Every day is a new beginning and a new trial. If "Plan A" fails, then you regroup, devise a "Plan B" and move on. If a situation falls short of perfection, do not view yourself as a total failure! Failure can only enter the arena when you give up trying and admit defeat.

The real challenge does not focus on our ability to complete a task or project but on our state of mind as we address any obstacle we face. A good attitude is perhaps our most powerful weapon against defeat and will ensure success. What happens to your worth is determined by your attitude. You are in charge of your attitude. Each and every day, you can choose how you will think, act and feel. With this thought in mind, we can discover the best in ourselves and others.

So now, let me ask you, *"Do you have change for a dollar?"*

TRANSFORMATIONAL CHANGE

"It is not the strongest of the species that survive, nor the most intelligent, but the one most responsive to change."
~ Clarence Darrow (1857-1938), American lawyer, ACLU leader

Heraclitus (c. 535 BC—475 BC) was a Greek philosopher known for his doctrine of change being central to the universe. Change is constant and inevitable—it is a universal law. Change is literally the only constant in all of science, and it will always be with us. It's natural. It's when people try to not change that it's unnatural—the way we cling to the ways things were instead of letting them be what they are, the way we cling to old memories instead of forming new ones. Change is constant. How we experience it is up to us. It can feel like death or like a second chance at life. If we loosen our grips, change can feel like pure adrenalin. By transforming ourselves, we can be born all over again.

When we understand and accept that change is necessary to free ourselves of harmful beliefs and attitudes, we can then begin the transformational process. Change is a continuous process of readjusting and refining ways of thinking and acting that everyone experiences throughout their lifetime. Take, for example, a child learning to walk. There's no single moment when s/he learns to do it. S/he staggers, struggles and falls until, finally, one day s/he takes a few steps...and falls down again. But they don't give up! They try again and again and soon enough they're off running.

There is an excellent bestseller book entitled "Who Moved My Cheese" by Dr. Spencer Johnson[42] that I believe simplifies the

---

[42] Spencer Johnson, *Who Moved My Cheese?* (New York: Putnam Adult, 1998). See Appendix A for a brief synopsis of the "Who Moved My Cheese?" story.

message that change is critical to our well-being. I also believe that without a strong sense of Human Worth change will be viewed and handled as an obstacle rather than the opportunity it provides us to strengthen our Concept of Self and maximize our potential.

"Who Moved My Cheese?" is the story of four characters—two mice (Sniff and Scurry) and two "littlepeople" (Hem and Haw)—living in a "Maze" who face unexpected change when they discover their "Cheese" is gone. When their cheese supply suddenly and unexpectedly disappears, their reactions reflect how we ourselves might react when faced with a similar situation (i.e., when our sustenance or comfort disappears). They will starve without their cheese. Their only hope to get more cheese is to venture out into the unknown paths of the maze. This dramatic change in their lives causes all four characters (whom we might recognize as ourselves when dealing with changes) to react uniquely; each of their responses represents a different and possible path open to each of us in our own daily lives.

The cheese is a metaphor for what we want to have in life, such as a job, a relationship, money, or health. While the maze represents where we spend time looking for what we want, the moral of the story is that our "cheese" moves all the time, but it's how well we react and adjust that makes us succeed or fail in life. Being adaptable to change will help make us happy.

When we change our course in life, we also can find and enjoy new "cheese." When we move beyond our fear, we feel free. Haw felt more alive because he took charge of his situation—he compared the danger between starvation and searching the fearful unknown—and decided that it was safer to search the maze (taking a risk). Whenever he felt doubtful, he imagined himself enjoying the biggest cheese in the world—and that kept him moving. He did wonder about Hem sometimes, hoping he would finally change his mind and look for new cheese in the maze. Old beliefs do not lead us to new cheese. The quicker we let go of "old cheese," the sooner we find "new cheese."

Noticing small changes early helps us adapt to the bigger changes that are to come. Sniff and Scurry had foresight and were proactive. They detected the change (the cheese was gone) and went out to start looking for the new cheese before the others were even aware that it had disappeared. Haw realized and learned that he might have found the new cheese sooner if he had gone out into the maze earlier. But better late then never! We must always be ready to face changes because it happens all the time in our careers and personal lives. It could be a new job or an old job with a different attitude.

Hem let the problem paralyze him. Too afraid to leave his comfort zone and go out into the maze (i.e., the unknown) to search for cheese, he resisted change, fearing that it would lead to something worse than starvation. He felt happy with his decision but never found a big and new cheese.

Sooner or later, each of us will experience change in our personal or work lives, but we all deal with it in different ways; our reactions to it come from the core of our existence—our Self-Worth, Self-Esteem and Self-Confidence. How we deal with change in our lives will impact our efforts to go after what we want in life. We don't have to fight change because it can help us grow. No matter how bad we think a situation is we can do well in changing times. Like Haw, we must adapt and let go of our old beliefs, habits and thinking; we must find new ones, move on and find our "cheese"— our sustenance and potential. People who turn their obstacles into opportunities for change will find a new source of comfort; those that remain behind, like Hem refusing to budge, are condemned to failure.

One of the most effective ways to bring about lasting change in our lives is to reflect on how we solve problems, make decisions and think creatively. To survive you don't have to be physically fit or super intelligent, but rather, you need to adapt to the changes around you, whether they are environmental or in attitude or perception. Unfortunately, it is the human condition that one does not always know how to adapt. Whether it be for food, shelter, rest, or emotional support, we constantly strive to do the best we can with whatever resources we have—our talents, skills and abilities, knowledge and beliefs. Some of us will lose confidence from mistakes that we make. Some of us face our everyday lives with dread—knowing that we may not survive because we lack the proper resources—not just money, education or physical strength— but that we don't have *internally* what it takes to adapt to change, that we simply may not be doing the best we can. Despite your mistakes, are you doing a good job? Is it the best job you can do? Your mistakes and the pain they cause teach you how to change your thought processes, behaviors and actions for the better.

However, the degree of success is irrelevant to feeling real Self-Worth—it is not the essential point. Some believe that the source of your real Self-Worth is only seen in the effort you put forth....in the force of life energy that keeps you going and trying.[43]

---

[43] Saundra Bubniak, *Human worth contingent on struggle to survive not cultural criteria,* http://www.examiner.com/holistic-health-in-detroit/human-worth-contingent-on-struggle-to-survive-not-cultural-criteria. Accessed Jan 2011.

You only get a glimmer of it while you are striving, struggling and trying to make the effort to succeed. When you no longer feel like carrying on and coping with life's daily challenges and you want to give up the struggle, you have lost the battle...and you will feel a sense of worthlessness.

Another avenue to bring about lasting change is to consciously improve our Concept of Self (i.e., our Self-Worth, Self-Esteem, Self-Love, etc.) but this is not something that can be developed overnight. One motivational author states "there is a growing body of research which indicates that it is possible to change the self-concept. Self-change is not something that people can will [e.g., "I will become better!"], but rather it depends on the process of self-reflection. Through self-reflection, people often come to view themselves in a new, more powerful way, and it is through this new, more powerful way of viewing the self that people can develop possible selves."[44]

For a great part of my life, I had such deep feelings of worthlessness that it was impossible for me to imagine just what feeling good about myself would be like. As a student labeled with behavior and learning disabilities, I struggled to learn. I was put in one of those special classes for troubled youths. My Self-Esteem was torn down and broken. I empathized with the deep feelings of worthlessness expressed by the many youth and parents with whom I worked while at the Tampa Bay Academy of Hope. I understood that there must be some way to feel positive about my own existence, but I simply could not imagine how it might be achieved. One thing I often wished for was to have someone who would help and guide me. I felt that no one could...instead, only simple admonishments or mindless brush-offs to "cheer up," or "get over it," "that's life" were the rule. It wasn't until the right mentors came along that I learned that my life could change for the better. They had such an impact on my success that I have included a section on 'The Importance of Mentors' in this book.

I used to find myself paralyzed with guilt because of my imperfections and looked for excuses *not* to change my situation or circumstance, believing that improvement was beyond my capabilities. Too often, this paralysis keeps individuals from doing positive things for themselves and others. Many are afraid to change and leave their comfort zones. Others may influence us to

[44] Robert E. Franken, *Human Motivation*, 3rd ed. (Pacific Grove, CA: Brooks/Cole, 1994), pp 439-443. Citation: W. Huitt, *Self and Self-Views*, Educational Psychology Interactive, 2009, Valdosta, GA: Valdosta State Univ., http://www.edpsycinteractive.org/topics/self/self.html. Accessed Nov 2010.

not change, wanting us to stay a certain way. They may talk us out of taking the steps needed to conquer and move beyond the limitations that hold us back from being the best that we can be.

It is critical to stop beating ourselves up emotionally because it doesn't change the past, nor does it change the future. It only makes the present miserable. In football, when you lose a game, there is only limited time to learn from the mistakes because you must then immediately move on to start preparing for the next game. If you have the willpower, then you can change. You are powerful beyond measure with an immense amount of potential residing deep within you.

Everything Must Change

"The only thing constant [in life] is change...Everything flows, nothing stands still."
~ Heraclitus of Ephesus (535-475 BC), Greek philosopher

There is a legend from India that tells about a mouse that was terrified of cats—until a magician agreed to transform him into a cat. That resolved his fear...until he met a dog. So, the magician changed him into a dog. The mouse-turned-cat-turned-dog was content—until he met a tiger. So, once again, the magician changed him into what he feared. But when the tiger came complaining that he had met a hunter, the magician refused to help. "I will make you into a mouse again. For though you have the body of a tiger, you still have the heart of a mouse." Sound familiar? How many people do you know who have built a fearful exterior, only to tremble inside with dread?

Life is a river of changes. We go through many phases of life—from childhood to adulthood to old age. Change is everywhere. The seasons change, the days of the week change, day changes into night and night changes into day, and the young become the old. Our careers, relationships, health, and economic situations can change dramatically. If we view ourselves as fixed, inflexible beings, then we will be threatened by change. If we view ourselves as growing, changing beings, then change, even negative change, is welcomed as a natural part of the growth process. If we do not learn to "go with the flow," then we risk being swept away and drowned.

Change is an inevitable part of life, and sooner or later, we have to come to grips with it. It causes a transformation that is based on one's values and priorities. Not having clarity about them can present an internal conflict between your feelings of worth vs. worthlessness. It's about moving from one state of being to another, to become different in some particular way. Change alters our lives; we become different in our essence and lose our original nature.

Change can have a profound impact on our Human Worth. My football-playing years were a life-changing experience. I felt the love of the fans and the approval of society. It gave me opportunities to see myself anew—equal to the others on my team. Football taught me how to focus, and I became a totally different person who now had Self-Confidence, Self-Esteem and Self-Love. But football also taught me how hard I would have to work to achieve something. It's a lot like life—when you get knocked down, it's how you get up and handle yourself that is important.

Many of us have been told or have come to believe that there is no need to change ourselves, that we should continue to accept our current situations and circumstances. This is a myth that has been perpetuated on us. Change helps us to grow as individuals and maximize our potential to overcome obstacles, change our community and the world, and bring happiness into our lives and the lives of our families and others.

Change is a process required to improve our current level of functioning. If you desire to transform your life, you must *change your way of thinking* in order to view your life differently. Because change is an alteration to our current life-style, it brings about unknown, ambiguous and uncertain breaks in our normal routines. As the process of change challenges our status quo, it becomes a threat to our security, beliefs, attitudes, and values. The way people perceive change is different from one person to another, depending on their personal beliefs. This can unbalance us and cause problems. Perceived with fear and dread, it unsettles the calm and peace we previously found comfort in. There are times when change forces us to utilize our inner, untapped resources and to adjust and cope with the unknown. Some people can be so set in their conditioning or conduct or are so content with their current state of being, that if they detect any hint of change, they begin to panic and take precautions to avoid change. People who resist change can be bossy, demanding and self-centered. They may remain in a state of being a victim of their everyday lives.[45] Your Human Worth will play a critical role and will continue to be the defining moment in how you change.

Some people need and desire change to feel vital and alive. For people who thrive on crisis and disarray, change can create

---

[45]Alfred Adler, *What Life Should mean to You* (London: Unwin Books, 1932).

new opportunities or a new way of life. Change can serve as a motivator to review the way they are living their lives and relating to others—to give them a chance to improve their relationships and their quality of life.

In my daily interactions with people, I hear over and over again *"Change is bad," "Change is unfair," "Life should be easy," "Why did this have to happen to me?"* Too often, people actively avoid change in their lives—they are frequently the ones who are very security-oriented and seek a set or patterned way of life for themselves. They act in a cautious manner in their personal and professional lives. Some, especially those individuals who suffer continuous reshuffling in unpredictable home or work lives, are willing to do anything to avoid changes in their lives. They resist discussions that will focus on areas needing change in their lives and withdraw from situations that might result in a need for change—*"If I ignore it, it will go away."* Those who resist change tend to associate only with people who support their beliefs and value systems which deny the need for change. They get angry with the people in their lives who confront them about the need for change—*"I want my life to remain the same!"* Despite setbacks and losses, those who refuse to change fantasize how their life can remain the same without any need to transform their lives.

Have *you* ever felt fed up and walked away because you don't like change? I have...and so I explored the possibilities of what may lie beyond the door of change. Little did I know that by opening that door, instead of giving up and staying in my comfort zone, I could alter my present thinking and existence and enter a new state of being. But what lies beyond the door of change is different for each individual. For some, it is giving up unpleasant thought patterns, bad relationships or unsatisfying jobs. Change could be as rewarding as a warm, sunny day on a beautiful beach in Florida.

Change helps us to grow, be more productive and learn from life's lessons by broadening our perceptions. It can alter a way of life in either a good or a bad way depending on how you approach or react to it. For every alteration or reformation that we undergo, either a positive or negative outcome will define and articulate the value and importance we give to our Self. It is more beneficial if we view and accept change in a positive way so that we can be invigorated and motivated to set goals of achieving greater accomplishments and perform at our highest potential.[46] Positive self-images can become self-fulfilling prophecies and allow us to achieve triumphs and victories in our lives.

---

[46] Ibid.

Oddly as it may seem, even positive self-images can have negative effects, especially, if they are too self-limiting. To some, a "C" grade is passing, but an "A" should be your goal if you plan to attend medical school. When I was in the second grade, my teacher held a speed contest in Math. I finished second in the class and was proud of myself. I believed that I was fast at solving math problems. I was so proud of being "fast at math" that it became a positive part of my self-image. Therefore, whenever I solved math problems, my goal was to work them faster than anyone else. Whenever I took a math test, I raced through the exam as fast as possible to be the first student to turn my paper in. This continued for more than five years, but I was blind to its negative effects.

One day, I wondered why my grades in math weren't as good as some of the "slow" students who turned in their papers last. I didn't realize that I made frequent careless errors because I didn't take the time to check my exams before turning them in. Taking more time conflicted with my self-image of being "fast in math." Eventually, I felt I was no longer smart enough; I "shut down" for a long time and didn't deal with any criticism well—to me, it was all destructive criticism. I was no longer motivated to study and perform well. Playing in the park was more rewarding than dealing with the rejections and criticisms belittling my earnest attempts to achieve. The child who fears that his mistakes would be detrimental and cause additional harm may not even try. At some point, my Human Worth came through and enabled me to decide that my grades were more important than this limiting self-image. I started to check my exams more carefully and not hand them in until the last minute. Limiting self-images undermine unconditional Self-Worth and undermine success in careers and relationships—we will fail to become all that we can be!

Changing one's self is an elusive task; it manifests itself physically, psychologically, socially, culturally, and spiritually. As the former Executive Director of the Tampa Bay Academy of Hope, I worked with youth and their parents who constantly struggled to make changes in their personal lives in order to find the hope and freedom to live happy and productive lives. These youth continually influenced and bombarded with negative pressures from their peers and society. Scared to be different, youth experiment with drugs, engage in inappropriate sexual encounters and believe that no one cares about them.

I have observed that underprivileged youth and their parents want to be valued and appreciated as human beings with Worth but are caught in a vicious downward spiral of hopelessness and despair. In reaction to their inability or refusal to change, many become depressed, angry, rebellious, defiant and disrespectful to others and themselves. I have witnessed youths using drugs to cope with the death of a loved one, missing their father or mother, the divorce of parents, or social and economic pressures because it was the only thing that helped to ease their unbearable pain. I have also seen youth attempt to take their life from either an accidental or premeditated drug overdose.

These and other experiences have expanded my personal understanding of change. I have realized that change is not a simple issue, but rather, it is made up of many components impacting everyone around us. The outcomes can be trivial and unimportant—or be of the most absolute significance. In the end, it all comes down to the individual's perception of change and how they choose to deal with it. The most important aspect of change is that we accept it and use it.

In the back of my mind, I often think of the 9-11 attacks on our country and the suffering that we, as citizens of the USA, experienced from the tragedy. The images on television forever changed our perceptions of our life in America and of the world. People were running and screaming as the twin towers tumbled to the ground and killed thousands of people before our very eyes. People were sitting in isolation with faces of profound sadness, fear and confusion. The 9-11 attacks forced us, individually and as a Nation, to confront a new change—because life as we once knew it was no more. This change to the American psyche was detrimental to our sense of comfort and security. But in spite of the tragedy, United States citizens and residents of all races, ethnic backgrounds and social/political/economic statuses united together. We put aside our differences and helped one another physically, emotionally, spiritually, and financially to overcome our national disaster. Our Human Worth was never more important nor was it ever more evident as it was during this horrific time.

Many theories exist that can help to explain why we need to or how we participate in a change to transform ourselves. To be the master of our own destiny, we must change our emotional state, not feel intimidated and feel liberated to change ourselves and embrace our Human Worth. Our willingness to educate ourselves about how to change and how to implement new skills and behaviors will reinforce and sustain our personal transformations. However, I must emphasize once again that until we embrace our Human Worth we will be paralyzed by the inevitable changes that confront and overwhelm us. Our Human Worth will guide us as we take the risks necessary for change. It will support us when we are confronted with fear.

Nelson Mandela stated in his inaugural speech, *"We ask ourselves—who am I to be brilliant, gorgeous, talented and fabulous? Actually, who are you not to be? You are a child of God. Your playing small doesn't serve the world. There is nothing enlightened about shrinking so that other people won't feel insecure around you. We are born to make manifest the glory of God that is within us. It is not just in some of us; it is in everyone. And as we let our own light shine, we unconsciously give other people permission to do the same. As we are liberated from our own fear, our presence automatically liberates others."*

It is crucial to acknowledge that no one can make you feel inferior *without your permission.* When we doubt our abilities, our intelligence, our Self-Worth, and our capacity to overcome obstacles, we risk the possibility of failure which can threaten to dislodge an already low sense of worth. It's a vicious cycle—if doubt, arising from low Self-Esteem, brings about failure, failure, in turn, further lowers your Self-Esteem with even more self-doubts. Change can involve a period of confusion and transition. Defense mechanisms have to be bypassed. We must overcome feelings of worry and anxiety which often arise whenever we even think of undertaking new challenges. In order to experience real change, existing "mindsets" must be dismantled and rebuilt.

If a drinking glass has been dropped and shattered into pieces, it can be fixed simply by gluing the bits and pieces back together again...or we can replace it with a new one. But when our Worth is damaged, it is very difficult to repair. We can't "buy" or replace our worth as if it were a broken object. Instead, our "new glass" must consist of making changes in our lives to replace our old ways of thinking so that we gain a new mindset and behaviors and move on in spite of what others may think. When we connect to our birthright of Human Worth, change can be like a rebirth or crossing the unknown—we attain a new equilibrium and can welcome change as an opportunity for growth and personal fulfillment.

The next section of this book will explain how various "obstacles to change" impact our sense of Worth and how we can overcome the challenges they present.

Obstacles to Change

"The difficulties in life are intended to make us better—not bitter."
~ Author Unknown

Obstacles are not dead-end streets but detours to change our day-to-day thinking. They are what make life interesting and overcoming them is what makes life meaningful. Think of them more as "challenges" providing you with the best opportunity to grow strong and survive in this changing world. Challenges can build and strengthen your trust in yourself allowing you to stand firm with courage against the winds of resistance as you continue your quest.

When we are confronted by obstacles, it tests our resolve. When you are tested, the testing brings clarity and shines a light on the task at hand. Is the goal you're aiming for what you really want? Do not be afraid to make choices in your life. You can manage any adversity and beat the odds. Be encouraged. Be positive; avoid or minimize negative thoughts. With a clear sense of Self-Worth and Self-Esteem, along with self-reliance and self-discipline, you can hold your ground and survive in today's society. Be optimistic, love yourselves unconditionally and be confident that nobody can stop you from overcoming any adversity.

It pains me to see that people are not willing to change because they are complacent and satisfied with their unfulfilling lives and not happy. When we feel a void in our lives, it gives us feelings of inadequacies and unworthiness. Change is challenging because of our conditioned thoughts, behaviors and beliefs.

If change is difficult for you, you may sabotage yourself and expect others to come along and save the day. With fear, negative thinking and a negative attitude, we convince ourselves that life is going to be awful and we will never be happy again. Because we have lost our power, passion and purpose, we feel we will be lost for the rest of our lives.

If your journey is like mine, you will struggle to change. I experienced extreme insecurity and anxiety when things important to me changed too much because I'm a person who likes comfort and control. It is important to remember that we cannot change everything in ourselves overnight. There may even be some aspect of ourselves that we may never be able to change without help from others, if at all!

THE POWER OF HUMAN WORTH

Fear of Change

"I learned that courage was not the absence of fear, but the triumph over it. The brave man is not he who does not feel afraid, but he who conquers that fear."
~ Nelson Mandela

Fear of failure and fear of success are negative, self-limiting beliefs stemming from low Self-Worth and self-doubt. When we fear that we don't measure up, might make a mistake or will be judged and humiliated, we are denying our Worth birthright and lull ourselves into believing that change is too challenging and does not merit the risk. We fear failure, but failure is great as a life lesson. The cost of failure is far lower than the cost of not trying. If you have to fail, do it quickly and learn from it.

Samuel Smiles, the 19th century writer and advocate of "self help," wrote:

"It is a mistake [to say] that men succeed through success; they much oftener succeed through failures. Precept, study, advice, and example could never have taught them so well as failure has done....We learn wisdom from failure much more than from success. We often discover what will do, by finding out what will not do; and probably he, who never made a mistake, never made a discovery."

Success is a long, long road, but failure is, too often, only a step away. Failure can be perceived as either a temporary setback or as a potential learning experience. When Self-Worth is strong, although fear may still exist, we no longer give it power to limit us from moving forward with our hopes and dreams in life. If we can dismiss distorted, fear-based perceptions that too often lead to inaction and stagnation, we will be able to create and sustain positive changes in our lives.

Your Human Worth tells you that you deserve success. Do not let the fear of failure prevail. Remember the story of the brothers Wilbur and Orville Wright? People ridiculed them for trying to invent what was to eventually become the prototype for the airplane. However, they refused to be dissuaded and continued in their quest until they had achieved their goals and attained the vision they both had created and believed in.

Success in the NFL

During the short time that I was a running back in the NFL, I was happy being a professional football player; it allowed me to see myself as a success. Comparing myself to former high school classmates who were not nearly as "successful," I thought that I was as talented as or better than other people. I had an inflated view of myself and only cared about success and acquiring the symbols of success. My total focus was on succeeding as a professional athlete to get everything I wanted—the image and the life style. I was just a 10th round pick, so I had to work even harder and take more risks. Here in the big-boy league, I had to prove that I was as good as the multi-millionaire athletes. Feeling inadequate, the increased risks I took resulted in increased stress—I feared failure and being looked down on by others.

Focusing on my personal success, I didn't listen to my wife's emotional needs. No one ever gave me a training manual for being married. Neglecting my wife, I drove a wedge between us. The burden and stress of being a pro became too much. I kept asking myself, "Why am I not happier?"

One thing that really bugged me was that my family back in Prichard, Alabama, was far less successful, yet they all seemed much happier. I had yet to learn a life lesson: that my happiness was not dependent upon my success in football.

Having a strong Self-Worth enables us to focus on taking the steps necessary to achieve and ensure success, but a fanatic devotion to success can be risky and uncomfortable. It is common for over-achievers to push themselves beyond the limits of their physical endurance and endure extra painful conditions; they rarely give themselves sufficient time to relax and enjoy what they do. They fail to lead well-rounded lives by overworking. The frantic struggle for achievement usually reflects a dire need to surpass others, to show that you are better than they are. But how much have others really got to do with you? If others have inferior traits, does that make you one bit a better person? On the other hand, if they surpass you in some performance, does that make you no-good? Only by arbitrary definitions are others better or worse than you. If you think that your "worth" as a human depends on how well your traits compare to those of others, you will practically always feel insecure and "worthless."[47]

If you frantically strive for success, you will feel anxious about failing or taking chances, beat up on yourself for making mistakes and avoid adventurous projects you would really like to attempt. By insisting on outstanding achievement, you will almost certainly make mistakes, feel depressed about them and then refuse "dangerous" tasks and put yourself down for copping out. Your compulsion to succeed dooms you not only to failure, but also to the fear of failing—which often is more life-cramping than failure

---

[47]Todd Atkins, *Earning Your Worth Through Accomplishment—Human Doing Instead of Human Being*, Baton Rouge Counseling, Jun 8, 2010, http://batonrougecounseling.net/earning-worth-accomplishment-human-human/. Accessed Feb 2011.

itself.[48]

When Self-Worth is lacking, success may bring another kind of fear—the fear of success. One of our deepest fears is that we may be inadequate. We may doubt whether we deserve happiness or whether sustained happiness is even possible. We dwell on the potentially negative reaction of our friends and family members—concerned about losing their love and acceptance due to envy, jealousy or resentment of our success. This need for external validation may cause us to compromise ourselves and our dreams rather than risk jeopardizing the acceptance we cling to. We may ultimately be afraid of unleashing our full potential, not because we fear we will fail, but because we fear our "power" and the outcomes of success. We worry that success may somehow taint us. These limiting beliefs tap into deep-seated self-doubt and often result in self-sabotage.

Restricting our abilities or withholding our brilliance truly serves no one. When we come from a place of non-negotiable Self-Worth and confidence, fear of failure and fear of success give way to faith in ourselves and the Universe. When we are able to tap into our inner resources, take risks, push past limitations, and forge ahead, the unknown will be perceived as a challenging, exciting adventure. Change becomes not something to fear, but worth embracing with confidence.

Fear defeats our Human Worth and limits our abilities to achieve our plans and goals by creating stress, panic and anxiety. Fear makes us feel inadequate. It discourages risk-taking and often manifests itself in indecisiveness. It suppresses our willingness to take a chance on fulfilling our dreams. Fear can cause us to turn our backs on our aspirations and leave our potential and dreams unfulfilled. Fear is a form of negative hope and paralyzes us from taking action. Fear of change predicts failure.

When my students at the TBAH didn't get good test grades and perceived themselves as academically-poor students, I discovered that testing then tended to become an intimidating and frightening situation for them. I often observed them "shutting down" with strong feelings of anxiety. The brain does not like pain! Anxiety is a signal indicating that there is trouble ahead and that you should avoid the situation. One way to avoid the situation is to run for the hills. Instead of running physically, my students "ran" emotionally and mentally by forgetting what they had learned, by using defenses such as avoiding test-taking altogether, and by acting out in the classroom. They sometimes paid tribute to their "Queen of Denial" who kept their fears out of their awareness.

---

[48] Ibid

The question is: "Are you ready to make the commitment necessary to change your negative thoughts and behaviors and increase your Self-Esteem and Self-Worth?" When we don't have a clear picture of how to move forward or have the confidence to do so, we are paralyzed with a fear of failure or fear of success which is all too often accompanied by or replaced with the fear of change. To overcome our fear of change, we must first learn to identify and understand our fears. We must then take action and work on them. When we discipline ourselves to manage fear and learn to adjust easily to change, we can become more effective in controlling our problems and renewing our lives.

Adversity

"When written in Chinese, the word crisis is composed of two characters. One represents danger, and the other represents opportunity."
~ John F. Kennedy

Adversity means trouble, difficulty or misfortune. It can be an obstacle in your path to change. Many of us have and will continue to experience challenges which may sometimes be described as setbacks. These situations occur when we lose our job, our business collapses, our relationships fall apart, or what we love and cherish is suddenly taken from us. But a setback is not the end of the road—it is also an opportunity to set us up for a comeback.

There will be no end to adversity in our lives, so we may as well get used to it. There's a hundred percent chance that we are going to experience ups and downs, and we will need to make emergency repairs more than once as we navigate through life. In my work, I am constantly confronted with the many rapid advances in technology—an obstacle that makes me feel powerless and overwhelmed in just keeping up! In our country, over fifty percent of married couples get divorced; some move on with their lives and some don't. Many remarry, learn how to take care of themselves, and are happy again. However, when your world is falling apart around you—have bills you can't pay, can't do things you need to do, experience heartbreak, and life is all "gloom and doom"—it's tough to remain optimistic.

Consider the compelling story of Nick Vujicic, who was born in 1982 in Brisbane, Australia. Without any medical explanation or warning, Vujicic was born without arms or legs; yet he did not allow his disability to lead him to a life of depression and hopelessness. He turned what could have been a life of tragedy into a life of triumph. Today, Vujicic travels all around the world sharing and encouraging others with his life story; encouraging others to use adversity as a challenge to accomplish those things that seem impossible.[49]

Family Problems

If someone were to ask me to describe my family in a single word, I would say it was chaotic. A family of 15 children was considered huge even in an era when large families were normal; birth control was not easily accessible in Southern rural areas. When my mother became pregnant, abortion was not an option, and so with each birth, she added another mouth to feed to our ever-growing family. As I look back over my childhood, the images that come to mind are those filled with all-consuming activity. It seemed to me at the time that I was the invisible child because I was just one in a multitude.

My family had two major handicaps which caused problems to seem insurmountable and the solutions distant and out of reach. First, there was a lack of education. Our family did not consist of college-educated people taught to evaluate solutions as well as problems. Second, and perhaps our greatest challenge, was the lack of knowledge for surviving in a city atmosphere. We were simple people with country ways and manners. When we moved from rural Thomaston to Prichard, near Mobile, we were ill-equipped to confront the problems that city-life brought. Therefore, it was truly a monumental task trying to survive from day to day.

When we lived in the country, we washed clothes in tubs and hung them on clotheslines to dry. When we moved into the city, there were no clotheslines and no washtubs. I remember carrying the clothes to the coin laundry, watching my mother as she washed and folded them, and then carrying the clothes back to the house. This was a weekly venture because we did not have the luxury of owning a washing machine—or a car for that matter. We walked everywhere we went. On some occasions, we relied on public transportation. Riding the bus was a luxury because money was always an issue and saving money for more important items, such as food, clothing or electricity, always took precedence.

If there was one thing our family became skilled in, it would be the art of moving. I remember living in several different rented houses on my way to adulthood. The houses may have been on different streets, and, sometimes, in different cities, but they were all the same: old-fashioned, shotgun-styled, wooden houses built high above the ground.

I remember my mother receiving monthly public assistance after we moved to the city. Unfortunately, the food only lasted for about two weeks. She would then buy

---

[49] Nick Vujicic, *Life Without Limbs*, http://press.lifewithoutlimbs.org/. Accessed Aug 23, 2011.

food on credit from the Jewish store in the neighborhood. This created a never-ending cycle of dependency. If she had known how to budget the food, prepare meal plans for the week and not waver from the schedule, she probably could have made the food stretch a little further. She did the best she could with the knowledge that a third-grade education provided. She lacked the ability to manage a household successfully, and no one was offering opportunities to break the cycle of dependency to people like us.

In our community, the one thing all of the neighbors shared was the struggle to make ends meet. As a result, there were occasions when I went to bed without eating dinner. Towards the end of the month, it seemed that every man was for himself. I learned how to be grateful for those meals I received at school. I do not blame my mother because I realize she was doing the best she could with what she had on hand.

Family trouble in some form or another was always on the horizon or lurking in the shadows waiting to make its unwanted appearance. Oftentimes, the problems centered on my older siblings. There were cases of spousal abuse when the mate of one or another decided the only way to settle an argument involved physical blows. The entire family would be swept up into the drama with lines being drawn in the sand.

All families have problems—the key to their solution is the manner in which the family addresses them. If we allow problems to control the family, it will be at the mercy of whatever comes its way. On the other hand, if the problems are faced by the family as a single unit, then solutions can more easily be found.

I find it remarkable that my mother was able to hold our huge family together at all. She was a source of strength and the calm center in the chaos that composed our family unit. If she had been wise to the ways of the world, things would have been different. She was a victim of the times and, while life was not easy for us, I realize it was much harder for her not being able to care for her family in the manner she wanted.

In my large family, with so many children and so much activity, it seemed that the children became invisible to the adults. My mother never knew about my dreams and aspirations. She had no idea that I had plans to make something of my life and that I would serve as an example to future generations.

If we stay focused on the downsides of what we see as all the bad stuff happening to us and to others, where will it lead? Life will always bring the good (the circumstances we like) along with the bad (the events we would rather not experience or deal with).[50]

---

[50] Steve Goldberg and Barbara Goldberg, *Finding the Upside: Practical Wisdom for Challenging Times,*

Adversities can beat you down and reduce your willingness to take responsibility for action or inaction. But that's OK. Everything happens for a reason. Scars remind us of where we've been; they don't dictate where we're going. The last thing you want to do is lose faith or hope because they are ways to keep your spirits up when your world is upside down. When we are at our weakest point in our mind, body and soul, faith and hope will help to overcome any obstacle. It is, oh, so easy to just give up and say, "Forget it!" The question to ask is "Isn't it worth it?" Isn't the dream you're pursuing really worth it? If through it all you can say "yes," then stay strong and keep plugging away.

Anger & Aggression

"He who strikes the first blow admits he's lost the argument."
~ Chinese Proverb

In 1999, the CBS TV show "60 Minutes" aired a special on juvenile delinquent elephants in South Africa. The matriarchs and other mature members of the herd, who function as the role models and keep the herd in line, were being killed off by poachers of ivory, among other causes. This left a high number of orphans who suffered psychological trauma as a result of their parents' deaths, many being killed or murdered in front of their young. Left without leadership, constant adult supervision and family structure, these orphans grew up to be overly aggressive and started to kill rhinos and humans which normally they would never approach. These rogue elephants had been terrorized by their environmental circumstances and were now terrorizing the inhabitants of those environments. They lacked the care and nurturing that their families would have provided.[51]

This aggressive behavior is mirrored in humans. There is no one in the world who is a greater mentor in a child's life than his or her own father or mother. Who is better to teach a child? A parent is truly capable of getting involved with their child's education, church, relationships, friends, and social activities. Similar to the animal world, if parents are absent, irresponsible or delinquent,

---

www.findingtheupside.org. Citation Steve Goldberg, *When Net Worth Becomes Self-Worth*, Life As a Human: The Online Magazine for Evolving Minds, Feb 22, 2011, http://lifeasahuman.com/2011/mind-spirit/inspirational/when-net-worth-becomes-self-worth/. Accessed Mar 2011.
[51] Elisa Nova, "Elephant Aggression on Humans and Rhinos," Opinion/Editorial, Nov 9, 2006, http://www.associatedcontent.com/article/80375/elephant_aggression_on_humans_and_rhinos.html?cat=9. Accessed Nov 2010.

then the worst of scenarios can occur with their young. Without proper guidance or role models to follow, the rates of juvenile delinquency and dropouts are substantially increased among neglected or abandoned youth. They affect entire communities.

Anger can be self-defeating. It hints at underlying personal unresolved issues, can lead to the loss of relationships, shows that you lack self-control, and does not solve your problems. Whatever has happened in your life, learn from it and then, with strength and a positive attitude, move forward. Limit your negative thoughts and replace them with more positive, constructive thoughts and assume the best in others rather than suspecting them of ill-intentions.

We can feel anger not only toward others but also toward ourselves (in the form of guilt). We will not be able to rid ourselves of the anger unless we can do the following:

1. *Accept* the effects of the actions of others. You cannot truly accept or forgive another until you have accepted all of the perceived consequences of their actions. Begin by working on accepting those. Find new routes to happiness—despite what they have done. Be grateful for the positives that you have. [52]The Alcoholics Anonymous serenity prayer is a proven tool which helps their members recover from addiction: "God grant me the serenity to accept the things I cannot change, the courage to change the things I can, and the wisdom to know the difference..." This acceptance is needed in order to move forward.

2. *Choose* happiness and health over anger. Are you holding on to your anger in order to punish the perpetrator? If so, your anger is harming you more than them—is that what you want? Don't let issues like unfairness, injustice or revenge become your central concerns.

3. *Develop* understanding and empathetic thoughts toward the perpetrator. We can use the same process of understanding, accepting and forgiving others that we use for ourselves. Deep understanding of the causes and empathy are the first steps to accepting negative effects of others' actions. Understanding and acceptance help reduce the blame and anger.

---

[52] Tom G. Stevens, *You Can Choose To Be Happy*, 2010, Chap 5, Part 3. Self-Acceptance, http://www.csulb.edu/~tstevens/h53accep.htm. Accessed Mar 2011.

Conditioning

"It is almost impossible for anyone, even the most ineffective among us, to continue to choose misery after becoming aware that it is a choice."
~ William Glasser, psychologist

The realization that our personality is the product of conditioning is an extremely important insight into the self-transformation process.

We all learn—in each moment of each day. Our past conditioning has taught us what we can and cannot do successfully and may even paralyze us when we think "outside of the box" and attempt to change. Our human nature and past experiences control and condition our needs and desires. Conditioning shapes, develops, and changes our perceptions of our worth, but our inherent, innate Self-Worth battles against those perceptions. Adapting to new beliefs, attitudes and behaviors will be difficult at first, but you can't afford not to keep trying with renewed and vigorous determination.

Our powerful subconscious mind plays a very important role in our decision-making and achieving what we want in life. Conditioned thoughts and behaviors are not always wholesome and consistent and may result in diverse conflicts in our life leading to unhappiness and sorrow. When we want to make changes in our lives, the past can be our own private monster crushing our happiness in the palm of its hand. Our subconscious can override our efforts to succeed. Where it has been trained by past experiences of failure, it keeps us from our dreams. Sometimes, it is the media, educational institutions or other external influences that have manipulated us to the extent that we limit our future endeavors. Whether or not it is frightening or difficult to take productive steps to overcome harmful learned conditioning, we must find ways to break away from it.

When we were young and impressionable, our parents were the major influence in our lives. They sent us many messages—some not communicated in a positive manner: "Be a lawyer when you grow up, and you won't have to worry." Repeated over many years, you then start to believe it and chose that career even though you wanted to be a musician. You do it to please your parents—not yourself. When you think a thought habitually or you make the same choices for so long that no other reality can be imagined or felt, you will make life choices to fulfill that destiny.

Some people choose to believe that their circumstances cannot change for the better. When experiencing a negative event, such as a career reversal or a failed relationship, they instead see it as a never-ending pattern of defeat. They over-generalize the situation by thinking the bad "always" happens or that the good "never" happens to them, and it depresses and discourages them. Likewise, they sometimes play mind-games by jumping to conclusions thinking things will turn out badly when there are no facts to support their conclusions. They fail to check things out or gather the facts and arbitrarily conclude that someone is reacting negatively towards them.

This is especially true for people who live without any hope of changing their lives. The behaviorist Dr. Abraham Maslow explained that we all do things that are dysfunctional to the health and happiness of ourselves and others. We are all only human and have limits to our knowledge, skills and resources. These limits can create dysfunctional habits that we may keep for our entire lives. However, our Human Worth is committed to growth and to our quest for self-actualization. It wants us to have a happy, productive life no matter what our past was like.[53]

Our conditioning causes us to create all kinds of wars against humanity—economic, racial, class, gender—because we are not taught alternatives or the consequences. Humans are capable of the kindest, most noble things, but without a sense of Worth, we are also capable of the most horrible and terrifying things. We hope for everlasting life but are always inventing new ways to destroy each other. To illustrate, our society sensationalizes and condones war. Movies condition our kids with sex, drugs, and violence. We've become conditioned to accept and even glorify the things that go against the very fabric of our society.

Conditioning can take the form of exposure to frequent negative name-calling and "put-downs" from parents or peers. We internalize not only their negative messages, but we internalize the persons themselves, the messengers. We have mental models of a little "mom" and a little "dad" inside us and their voices tell us how to behave. Our "inner mom" may be supportive, loving and understanding; but "mom" never learned to have fun, so she stifles your creativity. Our "inner dad" may be concerned about "being number one" or making a lot of money. He is intolerant of failure, yelling "stupid" or "idiot" whenever you don't do something perfectly—as the true story below sadly relates all too well...[54]

Abraham H. Maslow, *Motivation and Personality* (New York: Harper and Row, 1954), pp 155-156.
Citation: Tom G. Stevens, *You Can Choose To Be Happy*, Chap 5, Part 3, Self-Acceptance,
http://www.csulb.edu/~tstevens/h53accep.htm. Accessed Mar 2011.
[54]This story also closely mirrors the lives of some of my TBAH students, but is told here by Tom G. Stevens, *You Can Choose To Be Happy*, Chap 5, Part 3, Step 5: Overcome Your Fears Of Negative Labels, http://www.csulb.edu/~tstevens/h53accep.htm. Accessed Mar 2011.

One child's father had been psychologically abusive to her. As a young girl, she tried pleasing him and tried to meet his sometimes high, sometimes contradictory, expectations. If she did not do what he wanted, he called her "lazy," "bad," or "selfish." Once when she went out without his permission, he called her a "slut." She learned that no matter how hard she tried to please him, he would still berate her. So, she quit trying.

Consequently, as a teenager, she began to drink heavily, take drugs and generally led a wild life. She eventually left home and started working. With her new lifestyle, she hoped to get even with her father—she intended to hurt him by doing the opposite of what he wanted. She also hoped that her new friends and partying would help her drown out the inner voices that constantly told her what a loser she was. Those voices came from her internalized, dysfunctional father. She responded by sinking deeper and deeper into drug dependence and guilt.

Fortunately, she began to see that her drug-based lifestyle was making her more miserable than she had been as a little girl. She was haunted by guilt. She said, "I despise myself for wasting eight years of my life." Learning to accept herself and love herself was difficult: her internalized father still told her what a loser she was. Even though she had improved her life, those messages still haunted her.

Another part of her father was quite selfish. When she had lived with him, he wanted her to cater to him and be at his beck and call. Yet, he would disguise these selfish motives by saying he wanted her to learn "responsibilities," such as doing his cooking, laundry and housecleaning. If she didn't obey, he would say something like, "Look at all I've done for you, you selfish ingrate." The result was that she felt guilty and wondered if he really loved her.

What did her father really want from her? She finally concluded, the "good father" part of him really loved her and wanted what was best for her. He controlled her life thinking that he could ensure she would be moral, successful and happy.

Once she understood that these self-expectations (and guilt) were coming from her internalized father, she could examine them from her higher, more functional beliefs. One unrealistic expectation was, "I should never make a mistake. If I do, I should be severely—even eternally—punished for it." Another was "I am a bad person because I am an addict."

Positive self-talk was the only thing that helped her get lasting control of her guilt. She was convinced to acknowledge her Human Worth and to respond by saying to herself, "All people have great value—even addicts. I am not a bad person or a loser. I love myself unconditionally and am loved unconditionally—despite my past. I learned from it and could not be the person I am today without that experience."

She not only got control of her guilt, but she also got control of the deep anger she had felt toward her father (and most men). She had blamed him—as well as herself—for her years of unhappiness. She acknowledged, "Only because I understood and forgave myself, could I understand and forgive him." She started college, met a new group of friends, went to Alcoholics Anonymous, and began recovery.[55]

Conditioned behavior is not a dead end. If you have become conditioned to think of yourself as unworthy, weak and inadequate or believe that it is difficult to be successful, you will by nature experience that as your reality. However, you can alter and modify yourself for the better if you acknowledge and understand the conditioning that you experienced, learn how it has impacted your life and re-condition yourself to respond differently. When we realize that everything in life is a choice and that we choose our thoughts, we can change our choices. The negative habitual thoughts or conditionings that play over and over again in our heads (self-talk) can be changed to positive ones. The new positive self-talk that plays over and over in our conscious mind becomes our reality—as the subconscious mind hears this conditioning and accepts it as truth. We thus are re-conditioning ourselves; every time we have a negative thought, we can choose to counter it with a positive one. Our self-talk works the same way as repeating affirmations; saying or doing something repeatedly speaks to our conscious mind and as the thought remains as a constant, the subconscious mind will accept it as truth and create it as your reality. When we make the conscious choice to change our thought to positive affirmative thought, we have actually chosen what we are going to think. We have an incredible power within us to choose positive motivating words and thoughts. We have total control over our thoughts, which gives us the power to choose and recreate our destiny in ways that will make us happier, more responsible and more productive members of our community and society.[56]

"What happened in the past that was painful has a great deal to do with what we are today, but revisiting this painful past can contribute little or nothing to what we need to do now."

William Glasser, psychologist

It is important not to gloss over serious traumas that are experienced by individuals. Some people with Post Traumatic

---

[55]Ibid.
[56]Daniel K. DeFrank, "The Power to Choose," *New Times [Tampa, FL]*, July/August 2001.

Stress Disorder (PTSD) and related symptoms which need to be addressed should seek professional help. Childhood abuse—whether it be verbal, emotional, physical, or sexual—and alcohol or drug addiction are additional examples where therapy or a "recovery" process is required to heal. "Anonymous" groups and spiritual counseling can also address these issues.

Death

Death is not the end but rather another phase in the cycle of life and death. When a loved one dies, we fear that we will not be able to fill the void left by our loss. We can hold ourselves back and reduce our capacity to address the issue. What will happen? How can we survive? The death of a loved one can trigger a sense of doubt and can considerably weaken our will to connect to our Human Worth.

Dying To Understand

Some of my most vivid childhood memories are about death. Some people have the misconception that children are just little people. That is far from the truth. Children have a tendency to mimic adults even when they don't understand what they are doing. They are like little video recorders taking in everything around them and repeating what they have seen. It is those memories that they carry into adulthood.

I was traumatized by death by the time I was twelve and, as a child, did not understand why the people I loved went away and never returned. I now understand that when you are a part of a large family, death is far too often an unwelcome visitor. When it came, it left my mother and the other adults in my family emotionally spent. I remember family members dying and the effect their deaths had on the rest of us. Death was like a plague without a cure; it attacked often and stole the life of a family member, like a thief in the night. At one point, it seemed that I was going to a family funeral every month. People of all ages were dying all around me, and I was dying to understand why.

No one took the time to explain death to me. I tried to figure it out for myself. No one bothered to explain that dying was a part of life and that no matter how much I loved someone, that person was not immune to the outstretched arms of death. As I look back, I now understand that my lack of comprehension was not anyone's fault. It was the way children were treated during that era. Children were supposed to be seen and not heard. Adults felt children did not need explanations about certain things because they were too young to understand. That is why so many children from my generation grew up ignorant of things such as death, sex and drugs.

I distinctly remember when, in 1968, my baby brother, Lucas, died in my mother's arms. My mother was traumatized by his death. It seems that even now I can still hear her screams piercing the silence. As with all of the deaths, the other adults could not ease her pain, yet they tried to console her.

The tragedy of my older sister, Dessie, dying in a watery car crash with her 5-year-old son, Alfred, was the final straw that made me numb to the tragedy of death. I remember that rainy day so well. Dessie was riding with her son, my Aunt Ethel, and my cousin Arthur George when the car skidded out of control and landed in the river. I was told Dessie surfaced but would not save herself because she was looking for Alfred. We were told that she continued to look for him and disappeared repeatedly into the dark and angry waters until finally she did not come up anymore. Rescuers found her body the following day; Alfred was found further downstream two days later. Her final thoughts were that of saving her son. I did not understand at the time why she did not save herself. Today, I realize the power of a parent's love. This funeral was my first encounter with closed caskets. I never had the opportunity to see Dessie or Alfred, alive or dead, again.

Many of my older brothers were mixed up in the wrong things, and they often paid for their mistakes with their lives. My older brother, Lee, was mixed up in drugs and gambling when, in his late twenties, he was shot in the head by my cousin at point blank range during an argument while gambling. Everyone scattered after the shooting leaving Lee lying on the floor close to an hour before another older brother, Phillip, ran to get our brother Joe to help. I was told my cousin simply left the house where the shooting happened without a backwards glance. Joe took him to the hospital, but he was dead on arrival. He died abandoned and alone in less than an hour after being mortally wounded.

Lee's death in 1982 was extremely hard for me because I really admired him, and I was away at college at the time. As a child, I had never realized that Lee was involved in illegal activities. The Lee I knew took care of the family, put food on the family table and paid our bills. Lee protected us kids whenever we needed help or were in trouble. I looked up to him and felt safe with him. I spent many weekends with him and his wife who were like parents to me. His death divided my family right down the middle. Many of my relatives lived on the same street, and for years, one group refused to acknowledge that the other even existed. I do not remember what happened to bring them back together. However, I do know that my cousin was arrested and sent to prison which brought yet another tragedy.

One of my young cousins, Nate, had moved with his family away from Prichard to Detroit, Michigan. Three years later, he was stabbed to death after an altercation. Nate's death packed my heart in ice. By the time Nate died, I had no more tears to cry. He was my closest and best friend growing up, and we made plans for the future. We were supposed to share our dreams, and suddenly he was just gone out of my life. Facing his death was one of the hardest things I ever had to do. It was too hard to express my emotions, and I shut down. Somehow, I had the self-resiliency and came to understand that I must continue to live my life and pursue my dreams on my own without him.

As weird as it may seem, death had a way of pulling all my family members back together again and pointed out that we were all just mortal human beings, each with his or her own set of problems, dreams, and aspirations. I now understand that it's okay to let go of the people we love. Otherwise, we would condemn ourselves to live in the past. Eventually, I realized that I should not be afraid to love someone for fear that they would die and leave me.

Death continues to visit me often. Over the years, I have learned to accept it and am a stronger person for it. However, it was hard for me to attend funerals. When my favorite Aunt Betty, who helped raise me, died I could not bring myself to attend her funeral. In October, 1994, my 50 year old brother, Clark, had a seizure and died in his sleep. When I received the news I was hurt, but I was better able to cope with it because I had learned that it was okay to be sad. It was okay to miss him, and it was okay to let him go. I know that is what he would have wanted of me.

I have learned how to cope with death in my own way; while their body may be gone, I can keep that person alive in my heart through the memories of the good times we shared. I now choose to love the memories of my departed loved ones without letting their departure paralyze my future...I simply let go.

If we change our thinking about the negative aspect of death, it will decrease our fear and grief. Is there anything positive about death? For some, it is an end to the pain and suffering of a loved one. For Christians, it is the door into heaven. I believe that there is a bigger picture; that God is working everything out for the good of the universe. There will come a time when we will understand why people are suddenly taken from us or linger for years in pain before they cease to exist. God is working it out, and we have to trust in that. When we "bury" and "put to rest" any negative thoughts or feelings, that is a positive kind of loss that gives us a reason to celebrate!

Guilt & Shame

We have both an *ideal* self-image and a *perceived* self-image. The ideal self-image is what we want to be like ("*I should*"). The perceived self-image is based on our observations of what we are really like ("*I am*"). Guilt is caused by the gap between the ideal and the perceived self-image or, in other words, between self-expectations and self-perceptions, respectively.[57] The larger the gap, the more guilt we feel and the harder we find it to maintain a sense of worth. The *real* you is the person that you wake up with, the one you love or hate, the one you cry with, the "you" that, if all goes well, you will become. Until we can understand that our ideal self-image is always out of reach and is a standard that we can't meet, we will be out of synch with our real selves and the more we will suffer.

To overcome our guilt, we must reduce the gap between our self-expectations ("who I should be") and our self-perceptions ("who I really am"). We may have conflicting expectations from different parts of ourselves.[58] Ask yourself questions like, "What do I expect myself to be like?" "How does that differ from how I am?" "How are my beliefs, thoughts and actions different from what I expect them to be?" When we explore conflicting expectations, we may find conflicting answers to these questions. One part of us may expect to have a successful career while our other part may think that it will likely never happen. We can either change ourselves to become more like our self-expectations, or we can change our self-expectations (self-concept) to fit reality.

Many of us think that we don't deserve success, good relationships or have the right to question others. And we feel guilty when we do, thus making it hard for us to change. Some of us unjustly hold ourselves personally responsible for events that aren't under our control. This personalization leads to guilt, shame and inadequacy about how we contributed or caused the problem.

These self-imposed limitations can lead to fear and anxiety about our Human Worth. When we lack belief in ourselves, we convince ourselves that we can't do anything right or haven't achieved anything. We may become afraid that no one will care about us and that we can be replaced by others. We struggle and feel bad about our Worth. Consequently, whenever we doubt or fail to acknowledge our value in this world, we deny others from seeing the worth that lies within us.

When we fail to display Self-Esteem and Self-Confidence, others may then perceive us as inadequate or worthless, which in turn can cause negative reactions in us. Even worse, this vicious cycle is often perpetuated from one generation to the next. We blame ourselves for the problems in our lives as we continue a self-

---

[57] Tom G. Stevens, *You Can Choose To Be Happy*, 2010, Chap 5, Part 3, The Keys to Eliminating Guilt And Anger, http://www.csulb.edu/~tstevens/h53accep.htm. Accessed Mar 2011.
[58] Ibid.

inflicted cycle of guilt and ask despairingly, "Is this the life I am supposed to have?"

We must never deny our core values, importance, purpose, and meaning if we are to achieve our true potential in life. We must learn to release ourselves—and others—from real or perceived guilt about things we cannot control or change.

We all feel guilty for some reason from time to time, but when guilt leads to depression or feelings of worthlessness, then something needs to change. We feel guilty because we feel we should be better than we are. But it's difficult to get rid of guilt when we've been criticized all our lives. We can't suddenly stop feeling guilty, but we can start to let go and move on with our lives.

When we were small children, we trusted our thoughts and feelings and expressed them naturally without thinking about others or whether we should or shouldn't do so. But as we grew older we learned or, rather, we were conditioned not to express ourselves so freely. If your life was like mine, your parents and other adults manipulated and controlled you by modifying your behavior. This, in turn, made you feel guilty about your real Self and caused negative emotions about your Human Worth. In many family situations, when one member did something wrong, it didn't just shame that one family member—the whole family felt the shame.

However, the reality is that, after childhood, the more we allow others to manipulate or control our behaviors, the more we lose control of our Human Worth. We have to get to a point in our lives where we stop fearing what others may think about us. Our happiness and worth is not predicated on someone else loving and accepting us.

Some people love to tell us what we should and shouldn't do. They know how to push our insecurity buttons—that we should respect authority, that wives should obey their husbands or that we should always be polite to others. They remind us that we're not perfect, and we fall for it too often—just like when we were children when we looked around to see and copy what everyone else was doing. We often trust their authority more than our own worth. They sometimes go so far as to label us as a "failure," "fool" or "jerk" which are useless abstractions that lead to anger, frustration, and low Self-Esteem. Labeling is an extreme form of all-or-nothing thinking. It's irrational because the problem is not with the person per se (their character or essence) but with their thinking or behavior. You are not the same as what you do or say. Sometimes, we even attach negative labels to ourselves. Instead of saying that we made a mistake, we call ourselves a "loser." This only serves to make you feel hostile or hopeless about improving things and does not allow for constructive communication.[59]

Do not let others make you feel guilty for being too smart or not smart enough or for not being perfect. We all make mistakes. The truth of the matter is "you are what you are," and at the end of the day we're all doing the best we can with what we have. There isn't a person alive that hasn't hurt someone, whether intentionally or not. When our mistakes affect others, feeling guilty forever for those mistakes does not help them or us. You right the wrong if possible and tell them, "I am sorry," "I really didn't mean to hurt you," "Please forgive me," "I feel terrible about what I've done to you," "The reason I did what I did is...," or "What can I do to make it up to you and earn your trust again?" If the other person won't cooperate or accept the apology, you must let go of the guilt and move on with your life.

Isn't it ironic? But when we're successful in fulfilling their expectations of us, we fail ourselves by not valuing our own Worth, especially when their values conflict with ours. We shouldn't let others play God with us and allow them to impose their agendas upon us. Similarly, we shouldn't play God with them. The truth of the matter is that we should do what we know inside is morally right.

Sometimes, a little guilt is needed (e.g., when you do something that causes others hurt and pain)—it lets us know we have a conscience. However, too much guilt can be unhealthy and debilitating. Make a conscious effort to question your self-destructive beliefs and challenge yourself with new ways of thinking. When we live our lives according to socially acceptable values and beliefs, we have nothing to feel guilty about...and we honor our Human Worth.

Shameful Introductions

As a child growing up in Prichard, I had several experiences that left me with feelings of shame, guilt and confusion. In retrospect, I have come to realize that God has had His hand on my life every step of the way and saved me from harm.

My very first experience with sex was when I was nine, and like most children at that time, I was naïve to the ways of the world. I had not been as exposed to sex as my other family members were. One day, my cousin Nate and I were in my uncle's bedroom when his son entered the room, gave us a towel and told us to wipe our

[59]*Cognitive Distortions: Ten Forms of Self-Defeating Thoughts*, http://www.psychology-resources.com/library/Cognitive%20Distortions.pdf. Accessed Feb 2011.

butts and bend over. I was confused and did not know what to do. Nate was "country smart" and—thank God!—did know what to do. He grabbed my hand, yelled "Run!" and we ran like the wind. Nate saved me that day from an ordeal that could have conceivably altered my life forever. Many years have passed, but I will never forget that experience.

When I was 12, on my route to school, I had to walk past a certain house on a corner. The people who lived in the house were so nice that they eventually won me over. One day, they convinced me to come into their house. I left running for my life but not before a member of their household performed oral sex on me. This time, I was not confused; I knew what they did was wrong. I was so ashamed that I did not tell my mother what had happened. I buried it deep inside and that is where it festered until it manifested into a hatred for all gay people. Years would pass before I could unload my own guilt and recognize that I was the victim in this ordeal. Only after I was happily married did my wife help me understand that my anger should be directed at the person who took advantage of me and not at every gay person.

As a member of a large family, I often shared a bed with my older brothers. It was during my high school years that they would sneak their female acquaintances into the house to have sex. This should never have happened, but a parent could never be in more than one place at a time. But, perhaps, my most poignant experience with sex occurred when I was a junior in high school and was sowing my wild oats. This time, I was a willing participant. The librarian at our school became attracted to me. I was young, athletic and innocent. She earned my trust and took my innocence. I felt like a proud stud because I had an older woman. I did not realize at the time that she was only teaching me about the act. She failed to show me that sex without love is nothing more than intercourse. Nevertheless, the affair went on for two years and others around the school knew what was going on. I enjoyed the pleasures of the relationship and never gave any thought to the consequences, but they were forthcoming.

In our society, people tend to think that boys do not need as much protection as girls. That mistake is made far too often, and it is the child that pays the ultimate price. The affair went on with her buying me clothes and taking me out to places. It ended when she took me to a restaurant one day and with tears in her eyes, she professed her love for me. She said she wanted to marry me even though she was nearly twice my age. I did not know what love was and I certainly did not know how to deal with the situation. My solution was to avoid her at all costs. Avoiding her did not erase the damage she had caused in my young life. She was the first of many females who would lure me and give of themselves freely. After graduation, I entered college where I took advantage of all that my position as an athlete afforded me—sex available for the asking…and I asked a lot.

It was not until I met my wife at college that I learned the true meaning of love. She was a young, religious woman who had remained a virgin. We are still together today and the parents of two beautiful daughters. I am eternally grateful for her love.

I am also grateful that I overcame the guilt and shame from these incidents which could have changed my life forever. Had it not been for my cousin Nate, I could have fallen prey to a pedophile. Had it not been for the voice of God in my ear, I could have remained at that corner house and suffered something far greater than the shame of having oral sex performed on me by a man. Had it not been for my willingness to forgive those who inflicted hurt on me as a child, I could have remained shameful and embarrassed. My forgiveness allowed me to put the events behind me and move on with my life; my Human Worth demanded it.

Procrastination

Procrastination is a strategy to compensate for significant gaps in our Human Worth. Put simply, it is delaying or putting off the things you need to do. The lower our Self-Esteem, the greater our procrastination. It can be disruptive to our health and happiness. For those of us that had strict and controlling parents, procrastination is one of the few means we had to rebel against our parents' control—procrastination was our way of attacking our family values. Overcoming procrastination can be very difficult because of the root causes which, all too often, are unrealized or, perhaps, denied.

There are many reasons why we put off doing certain things, but knowing the true causes may not even help. We may fear failure (or success), disapproval of others, believe the task at hand is too complex or too time-consuming, etc. We can reflect back to our childhood where the expectations and criticisms of our parents and others formed what many call "socially-prescribed perfectionism."[60] This fear of failing to live up to their ideals can unknowingly cause us to procrastinate and avoid the possibility of disappointing others or suffering their disapproval.

Sometimes, there is a neurobiological basis to procrastination. Individuals with ADHD typically have executive

---

[60]Jeffrey J. Klibert, Jennifer Langhinrichsen-Rohling, & Motoko Saito. "Adaptive and Maladaptive Aspects of Self-Oriented versus Socially Prescribed Perfectionism," *Journal of College Student Development* 46:2, (March/April 2005): 141-156.

functioning deficits including difficulty with task initiation, which essentially appears like procrastination to teachers and others. This is biologically-based in the pre-frontal cortex and there is much research on this. These individuals will have more of a challenge and have to work harder in this area in order to transform themselves; it should not be an excuse for giving up or copping-out![61]

If we delay or avoid doing things in a timely manner, we will struggle with change. If procrastination is persistent and habitual, it can become self-destructive. For example, when we delay getting out of a bad relationship, we endure not only heartache but an abused sense of worth; when we put off furthering our education, we limit our economic and social opportunities. The more we delay changing our behaviors, attitudes and beliefs, the less likely we are to achieve our goals and dreams.

Overcoming procrastination involves developing a plan of action. It is important to keep the plan simple. Start with the less time-consuming items first so that the achievement motivates you to continue. It is also important to use time management to set priorities and deadlines and monitor which tasks on your plan are being accomplished. Most of all, overcoming procrastination starts with believing in yourself and your ability to make it happen!

Rejection & Disapproval

We all battle with the fear of rejection or the loss of approval from others. Too often, we bank and invest our Human Worth on their approval. We convince ourselves that without their approval our beliefs and behaviors must not be up to par and are "unworthy." In this way, their rejections injure our Self-Esteem and Self-Worth. We become afraid of confrontation and standing up for ourselves not only because it could result in rejection and disapproval but because it could also cut away at our sense of worth.

When we are too concerned about what others may think of us and believe success cannot be achieved without the "permission" of others, we will suffer from a lack of Self-Worth caused by the false belief that we cannot "make it" on our own. I used to struggle with the fear of letting go of people whom I thought had my and my family's best interests at heart—people whose approval I thought I needed. With the strong sense of worth that I have today I know

---

[61] Contributed by a personal friend, Angela T. Sheble, Ph.D., Florida Licensed School Psychologist.

that I don't need others' permission or approval to validate who I am or who I will become. However, I am mindful to not cause others to feel rejected or disapproved of; I try to always encourage and motivate people to be true to themselves. In this way, they can more easily connect to their Human Worth.

If we change our behavior to be true to ourselves, we may fear that we will hurt or disappoint those we love and care about. We may fear that we are being disloyal or unfaithful, especially to those who we believe need us—who we think could never succeed or survive without our support. Some (pastors, leaders) have many people to guide or help and may feel obligated to take care of them all. I think this guilt must be seriously addressed and overcome. When we don't allow our loved ones to struggle with their own challenges, we prevent them from experiencing the lessons that life teaches and we fail to give them the "tough love" which would allow them to make the changes needed to maximize their true potential.

Life is hard enough without worrying whether others don't or won't like or love you, will judge you badly or never do anything for you. Some people will reject and be angry with us no matter how perfect we are. Regrettably, that's just the way life is and you might as well get used to it if you intend to stay connected to your Human Worth.

Victimization

When we were children, our parents controlled us and told us what to eat, how to sit, what to say, when to sleep, and so on. We were not free to internalize our own actions or goals. Even as adults, we depend on or are influenced by external control, but too many people distort this into a blaming game—blaming others for their misfortunes.

How many times do you think you've been victimized? Some people continually think and live as if they are victims. They do not take responsibility for their actions or inactions and blame others for their problems.

The mentality of victimization is a big problem because it perpetuates a sense of worthlessness, uncertainty, hopelessness, and despair which are all major obstacles to change. If we are too poor, we can blame the economy for our not having a job—and we give up trying to find a job or organization to help. If we get fired from a job, we may blame the supervisor who "had it" with us—and deny that our poor performance or constant lateness to work was cause for dismissal.

We cannot make conscious changes for the better if we do not believe *it is up to us* to make adjustments in our lives, but believe that it is others who must change or "right the wrong." We are in denial—everyone else but us is the problem. We reason with ourselves, justify and come up with good explanations and make excuses for our actions or shortcomings.

A student receiving poor test grades may, for example, blame the teacher for poor teaching, trick questions or a bad attitude. The fact that sometimes teachers are poor instructors, write trick questions or have a bad attitude only makes our excuses work better. We must stop pointing our fingers at our parents, boyfriends or girlfriends, husbands or wives, children, etc. for our problems; we must assume responsibility and get on with changing our lives for the better. We all have a choice in everything we do.

Victimization takes another form when we blame our "human nature." We are all only human and have many limits to our knowledge, skills and resources. People often justify their unacceptable behavior by stating, "Well, that's just my nature," assuming the belief that our imperfections are too difficult to confront or overcome because we are subject to our human nature. This school of thought robs us of our Human Worth and the opportunity to change. There's another perspective we can take. Instead of talking about human nature, we can talk about our Human Worth. Thinking about ourselves as individuals with Self-Worth, instead of creatures defined by our nature, gives us personal power.

When we free ourselves from obstacles to change, we can elevate our state of mind. It's not comfortable letting go of our negative attitudes, feelings, habits, and behaviors, but doing so will allow us to make the inner transformation to connect to the peace and Human Worth within ourselves. Real change requires us to accept personal responsibility for our life and make the necessary changes that will empower us. Don't settle for having a merely interesting life, the key is having a meaningful one. You are on a voyage to discover your Human Worth and are travelling uncharted galaxies to reach Planet Change.

Take Action

"Be the change you wish to see in the world"
~ Mahatma Gandhi (1869-1948)[62]

I did not stand by when my community came to me looking for answers when questions about racial injustice arose over the killing of innocent young black children by a white teacher. I took action and promptly arranged to hold a town hall meeting to let the voices of the people be heard.

The News Report:
On the evening of March 31, 2004, four young siblings were struck in a hit-and-run car accident in Tampa. Two died. On Aug. 30, as part of a deal struck with prosecutors, former Tampa teacher Jennifer Porter admitted her involvement in the accident and pleaded guilty to leaving the scene of an accident involving death.

The Sentence:
Porter served no time in jail. She was sentenced to three years of probation, two years of community control or house arrest and 500 hours of community service.

The Key Players:
- Jennifer Porter, 29, former Muller Elementary School dance teacher, lives in the Land O'Lakes area with her parents.
- Bryant Wilkins, 13, was fatally struck just before his birthday when he was crossing the street with his 3-year-old brother, Durontae Caldwell, who was also killed.
- Their siblings Aquina Wilkins, 8, and LaJuan Davis, 2, were seriously injured but survived the accident. Aquina has had two surgeries to repair a broken femur. LaJuan recovered physically, but it is too early to know if he suffered brain damage.
- Lisa Wilkins, 30, mother of the four children, now lives in Land O'Lakes.
- Barry Cohen, 66, the attorney Porter's parents got to defend her.

---

[62] Mohandas Karamchand Gandhi (commonly known and addressed across the world as Mahatma Gandhi) was a major political and spiritual leader of India and the Indian independence movement. He was the pioneer and perfector of Satyagraha—resistance through mass civil disobedience strongly founded upon ahimsa (total non-violence).

"They Came Looking for Answers"[63]

The frustration was evident as 200 people,[64] mostly black, turned out for a town hall meeting to discuss the Jennifer Porter case. They were angry and sad, accusatory and befuddled. Panelists included the state attorney, Porter's attorney, a public defender and NAACP representatives…

…Almost a month since a white woman was sentenced to community control after pleading guilty to an accident that killed two black children, about 200 people— most of them black—packed into a Tampa church to ask what they think are unanswered questions.

Why was Jennifer Porter never charged with vehicular homicide? Why wasn't her father prosecuted after admitting he washed blood from his daughter's car? What did Porter's attorney mean when he told TV cameras recently that black leaders needed to stand up and tell the community the truth?

"We are not here to retry the Jennifer Porter case," said James Evans, executive director of the Tampa Bay Academy of Hope, who organized Thursday's three-hour town hall meeting at Beulah Baptist Church. Rather, he said, the purpose of the meeting was to address weighty questions about racial disparities in the justice system to the people who know them best: the prosecutors, attorneys, law enforcement officials and black leaders involved in the case.

Porter, a 29-year-old teacher, pleaded guilty to leaving the scene of a March 2004 accident that killed Bryant Wilkins, 13, his brother Durontae Caldwell, 3, and injured Aquina Wilkins, then 8, and LaJuan Davis, then 2.

On Nov. 5, she avoided prison time, sentenced instead to two years of community control, three years of probation and 500 hours of community service.

"My question to you is: Why wasn't my son afforded the same opportunity Miss Porter was?" asked Kadani Rivers, a black woman whose son, 16, has been prosecuted several times.

[The state attorney] fielded many such questions from people who said that if Porter had been black, the outcome would have been different, the prosecution would have tried harder.

[Porter's attorney]…who had said…that he wouldn't attend the community event, took the microphone several times. Black attorneys failed to tell their community the case for vehicular homicide wasn't there, he said. And, he said, all the facts

---

[63]Rebecca Catalanello, "They Came Looking for Answers," *St. Petersburg Times* [FL], 2 Dec. 2005, http://www.sptimes.com/2005/12/02/Tampabay/They_came_looking_for.shtml. Accessed Aug 24, 2011.

[64] Author: This is not true! There were over 800 present with 200 of them outside the building. I was there.

hadn't come out: The children, retreating from the path of a white van, backed up into Porter's lane, he asserted.

"It wasn't like she mowed them down," he said to boos and yells.

"She did!" a man shouted.

[The state attorney] said Porter's parents had been given immunity from prosecution, because they needed them to confirm that Jennifer Porter was driving the car. Evans counted the meeting a success, an opportunity for people to talk about their frustrations and give voice to their concerns. "This isn't just a black issue," he said, "it's a community issue..."

Action is defined as a process of doing something. Our worth comes greatly from feeling that one has taken a sufficient degree of useful and valid action in the world. To me, taking action is as simple as breathing. In the Jennifer Porter incidents above, I saw the need, and I responded.

We all have experienced things that have challenged us and will continue to challenge us to the limits. People in authority or with power over us, or even our parents, can oppose and adversely influence our struggle to change. However, even as life challenges us, we must press forward and rise above adversity. It is up to us whether or not we prevail.

Warren Buffett once stated, "someone's sitting in the shade today because a long time ago someone planted a tree;" a small action can have great results.[65]

Dietrich Bonhoeffer[66] says that action springs not from thought but from a readiness for responsibility. When you are ready to do something in your life with energy, motivation and passion, you can act. Just remember that energy stored in your body is like gun powder in a bullet. All you have to do is pull the trigger and feel the trueness of purpose. When you fire your gun, it will turn your bullet intc a powerful explosion of active energy. Taking action is like the burst of fire from that gun.

However, taking action is only a step on the road to transformational change. Experts say people go through several stages before they really change.[67] The first phase is thinking about it; for example, when the community came to me with their

---

[65]Warren Edward Buffett, Chairman of Berkshire Hathaway, is an American investor, industrialist and philanthropist. He is widely regarded as one of the most successful investors in the world. Quote is cited at http://quotationsbook.com/quote/461/. Accessed Aug 2010.

[66] German Theologian, 1906-1937, *The Cost of Discipleship* (New York, NY: Touchstone, 1995).

[67] Anthony Robbins, *Awaken the Giant Within* (New York: Free Press, 1992).

concerns over the Jennifer Porter case, I first thought about the need, consequences and the outcome before arranging a high profile town hall meeting to provide a platform for their issues and frustrations. If you wanted to lose weight, your first step may be to mull over joining a gym or reading articles about weight loss before actually joining a gym.

In the second stage, you make a decision to take action. For example, making a New Year's resolution is making a commitment to change. Making a decision indicates that you are ready to put a plan into motion.

After seeing the hurt and the perceived injustice in the Jennifer Porter case, I became even more compassionate about the social ills in my local community. Jennifer Porter did not wake up that morning wanting to kill innocent children. My compassion for both the schoolteacher and the victims' mother moved me to call the local media, circulate flyers, send emails, and hold that town hall meeting. I decided to help ensure that racial tensions did not escalate in my community.

Before embarking on the journey to change your life, let's narrow down the number of steps to these four key ones:

Step 1—Identify your Motivation
Step 2—Define Your Goals
Step 3—Create an Action Plan
Step 4—Track your Progress

Step 1—Identify your Motivation

Why do you want to change? For example, if you want to play football, is it because you like to win? Be in the limelight? Be part of a team? Once you know your motivation, your goals will be clearer and more concrete. Goals need to be relevant to something deeper and more meaningful to you. Motivation is the energy you need to steadfastly move forward towards your goal.

Step 2—Define Your Goals

The second step should be to set and define your goals. Goal setting is mandatory. In order for something to happen, it's important to set a valuable goal that enhances your focus. Goals are like putting an apple in front of a horse to make it move forward. Without goals, you are likely to wander off course. Why? It's hard work. It requires time, soul searching and discipline.

Goals provide direction and help to shape our dreams and aspirations, help us set priorities and work within a time frame.[68] Goals must be clear for yourself and others. They have to be valuable and meaningful to you. If a goal is trivial, it will seem unimportant and become buried under the crush of our daily struggles.

Select the improvements you'd like to make and create a series of goals necessary to implement those changes. Set short and long-term goals. Visualize them in order to make them seem more possible and real. Each time you accomplish something you set out to do, you'll get a good feeling and will be motivated to try, again and again, with renewed vigor and determination. This feeling cannot be taken away from you. You don't feel good because you are better than someone else; you feel good because of personal achievement.

State your goals in the past tense, as if you have already achieved them and then commit to them. If you have too many goals, you might become overwhelmed with all there is to do. You can literally paralyze the change process into a state of inaction. You've got to prioritize your dreams and goals to increase your motivation to go in the right direction. On the other hand, too few goals will not be comprehensive enough to make a real difference. For example: Your goal may be: "In one year, I want to build a house that will cost $350,000." This is a specific, clearly defined goal with an essential end in mind. What do you desire the most? Is it realistically possible? Your future is determined by you—make it count!

Do you remember the story of "The Little Engine That Could?" There's a trainload of truth behind that children's story. People are more likely to reach their goals if they *believe* they can do it...if they think they can, if they think they can, if they think they can. Once you've set your sights on an outcome, don't doubt your ability to achieve it. You will eventually grow to feel comfortable with the new ways of thinking, behaving and succeeding; they will become as natural as breathing. For this to occur, goals have to be attainable, practical and balanced. A goal that blocks rather than facilitates progress will also hinder our plans. For example, if the goal requires too many resources or is too difficult-to-obtain, then it will delay or hinder your progress. Goals should be challenging but realistic, organized and detailed. Write them down to remind you of what you really want to achieve with

---

[68] JoAnn Dahklloetter, *Your Performing Edge: The Complete Mind-Body Guide for Excellence in Sports, Health and Life* (San Carlos, CA: Pulgas Ridge Press, 2004).

all of your heart, and they will become a part of you. Unwritten dreams remain vague and won't give you the passion it takes to fulfill them. Written dreams are more concrete and specific, thus we are less apt to wander off course.

Break down large goals into smaller, more manageable ones. If the goal is too large or complex, it will be put off under the perception that it will take too much time or effort—that it cannot be completed in a reasonable or satisfactory time frame. Don't train for a marathon (26 miles) when you first need to train for a 5K (3.1 mile). Once you achieve your goal, you can then set a more challenging one. Achieving your goals takes diligence and discipline, but even small changes can produce significant gains in your quality of life. Here are some examples of "small" goals for you to achieve:

- Smile more
- Apologize to people when you have hurt or ignored them
- Keep a calendar of birthdays, anniversaries and other significant dates
- Be more friendly, positive and optimistic when you meet people
- Accept people as they are, not as you would like them to be
- Treat those you are close to with courtesy, be sure to say please or thank you
- Speak words that uplift the spirit—an encouraging word can go such a long way
- Build trust by admitting mistakes
- At work, focus on people's good qualities, seek feedback on your performance, ask if you can help others when you are caught up, limit outside distractions (such as phone calls from friends), and always be on time and in proper attire
- Increase your tolerance for different viewpoints

For goals to be most effective, they should also be SMART—Specific, Measurable, Attainable, Realistic, and Time-oriented.[69] For example, instead of saying "I'm going to make the pro-football team," specify "I'm going to train and exercise 3-4 hours every day until I can run 5 miles and bench press 225 lbs." Setting specific and measurable goals provides the feedback to tell you how well you are doing.

Finally, to make changes in your life you must make the commitment to yourself to complete each goal. When you have successfully completed a goal, it reinforces your self-image and

---

[69] Ibid.

esteem and provides the motivation to continue on to the next goal. Completing a goal will give a core of confidence, worth and esteem that you can build on. After you have reached a goal, you must continue to set goals in order to move forward in life. Set more challenging ones in order to move forward in life. It's important to do things that you're not comfortable with. Push yourself to do things that you've never done before. No one decides if you will be successful in life but you; you decide whether or not you will achieve your goals. No one can guarantee that you will have a good life but you.

Step 3—Create an Action Plan

"Action expresses priorities."   ~ Mahatma Gandhi

You have unlimited potential, but you must make a plan before you take action! A vision without a plan is more like a hallucination. You can begin to make meaningful changes in your life by creating a new plan for yourself. Action without a plan is like building a house without a blueprint or baking a cake without a recipe. The creation of a step-by-step action plan is crucial to obtaining your end result. However, even the most perfectly constructed and thought-out action plan is of no consequence if it never comes to fruition. Completing one is a precursor to success. Practically speaking, to benefit yourself, any actions you take must be considered correct, proper and acceptable to your Self, but they must also be useful and valid in the world.

- **Action #1**
  It is vital to actively choose to surround yourself with worthwhile individuals. You were never meant to do everything by yourself. Sometimes, you need to have people around who will love and encourage you. Surround yourself with them, as their caring and affection will help you through the tough times in life. Unworthy people must be avoided because they will drag you down and make YOU feel worthless! This is not a matter of ego or whim—it is a matter of survival. For this reason, I encourage people to avoid those who put them down or abuse them or otherwise depress and sadden them.
  Find a compassionate mentor who will help, guide, lead, strengthen, and challenge you to become all that you can be. Find a dedicated mentor who will commit to teaching you a new way of thinking and behaving and who will inspire and motivate you to try to be the best that you can be. You want a mentor in your life who will tell you the truth and be real with you. You

want to have someone who has high moral standards, who will not judge you, but accept you for who you are. You don't need the approval of others, but mentors do validate your worth and you are supported by their love and encouragement.

- **Action #2**

    Knowledge is power and creates inner certainty which builds confidence. Whenever you feel anxious about the changes you want to implement in your life, there are many options to gain the knowledge you need to support you in your efforts, such as self-talk, social interaction, help from support groups, mentors, tapes, seminars, and books.

    Read more. Through reading, you will gain new knowledge and understanding, and it may help you to clear whatever may be blocking your thinking. Books allow us to learn about those people who fought fear with courage and succeeded in life. Take courses and familiarize yourself with information in the area in which you are passionate about. If you can't get knowledge or work-experience in your desired area, then volunteer in that environment to learn all that you can about it. For example, I volunteered in non-profit organizations to learn how they were operated because I wanted to start one to help others.

    Your knowledge about yourself, i.e., how you perceive yourself, is critical to the way in which you will take action. If you believe that you are well-informed in what you are inspired to do, then you will feel capable and confident that you can achieve your desired goals. By being confident and building on your strengths, you can become effective and creative.

    Learn from your past! Address your past fears, shame, inadequacies, or embarrassment. Your Self-Esteem will rise in the knowledge that much of what hinders our progress to change originated from negative conditioning we received very early in our lives. What we were told then seems to stick with us and influence our decisions and actions throughout our lives. Realize that not everything we were told as kids was the truth. It is very difficult to free ourselves from this conditioning which stores itself in our subconscious, but we can turn the negative aspects of our lives into positive ones. Knowing this gives us the potential to move beyond the hurt, pain and disappointment of our past, but you must also muster a fighting spirit and the courage to address, engage and confront the painful images and feelings that we keep buried and hidden deep inside our souls...and let them go. Move past the time when your worth suffered. Bring yourself to the present where you can resolve deep-seated issues by acknowledging them and moving on. However, when you neutralize undesirable conditionings you must also initialize the formation of new wholesome ones.

- **Action #3**

    At every waking hour, visualize or imagine positive images. Newly acquired knowledge enables you to change your mental pictures and will help change how you see yourself and your surroundings. Start to change your old, disempowering images and replace them with positive ones. Recall a time when you felt good about yourself, when you felt okay with all your faults and failings, in spite of others' opinions. (This powerful technique is also used and recommended in cognitive-behavioral therapy.)

    To help focus on the positives in your life, you must love yourself unconditionally. It's important to take three to four minutes every day to look at yourself in the mirror and tell yourself over and over again how much you love and respect yourself. Give yourself a new look by going out shopping for a new wardrobe, get a new haircut or pamper yourself by going to a spa. These actions can make you feel good about yourself. A good appearance can also have a very positive effect on your confidence and Self-Esteem.

    Being at peace or at one with yourself is also very important to being positive. Learn techniques for both getting in touch with your feelings and for nourishing your soul (nature walks, prayer, meditation, etc.) Discipline yourself to take some time out of each day and spend it in solitude. Spending time alone allows you to reflect, calm the mind and get to know yourself.[70] We all need some "Me" time! Pretty soon you will find yourself feeling positive and acting with more confidence.

- **Action #4**

    Do something about your energy level; physical activity will make you feel more energetic, awake and alert as well as make you sleep more easily. Walk in the fresh air briskly for fifteen minutes every day, eat healthier foods, set a schedule and stick to it. Consult your doctor to see if you can start a training program to help improve your physical fitness and

---

[70] Saundra Bubniak, *Human worth contingent on struggle to survive not cultural criteria*, http://www.examiner.com/holistic-health-in-detroit/human-worth-contingent-on-struggle-to-survive-not-cultural-criteria. Accessed Jan 2011.

reduce stress. For example, use breathing and muscle relaxation techniques that systemically tense and relax groups of muscles (forearm, upper arm, so on) separately and then later combine them so that you are able to relax the whole body at once. Such techniques allow you to become more composed and calm. A lack of exercise and having a diet of mostly junk food does nothing for your confidence and makes you lethargic and unmotivated. Fatigue can drain your energy and increase stress. When you are tired and run down, it is important to get the proper rest. Throughout my life, I have trained my mind, body and soul to respond to my daily challenges. Being mentally, physically and spiritually fit makes me feel good about myself and gives me the motivation and confidence to achieve my wildest dreams.

These four action steps form the basic Action Plan to make you feel a lot better about yourself and instill in you the belief that you are not just some worthless and inferior human being. It is amazing what a fresh makeover can do for your Self-Worth—you will exude being that new person. Trying new challenges will help improve your confidence. Your Self-Worth will rise, and you will feel great about yourself. People will be drawn to you. I find it fascinating that when, combined with a good action plan, someone has the desire, commitment and willingness to improve, they find themselves transformed and connected to their inner Worth. They succeed, prosper and enjoy the best that life has to offer because they know that they deserve it.

For the first few days of implementing your plan, it's easy to do so with enthusiasm and anticipation. Then, after the initial rush of excitement wanes, we begin to find excuses for slipping back into our old habits. We all have 24 hours to accomplish our tasks each day, but many of us waste our days by not using our time wisely. Using your time wisely is simply making the right choices about how you will tackle your goals, i.e., by being productive and effective by selecting the best goals from all the possibilities available and then acting on them. We have plenty of time to do everything we really want to do. There are many people who are even busier than we are, but still manage to get more things accomplished than we do.

Step 4—Track your Progress

You must plan your work and work your plan. To assess how you're doing, it's important to track your progress. Track what does and doesn't work in your plan by entering them in a "Power of Human Worth" journal. When you track your thoughts and ideas, they become clear and serve as a guide to finding your true essence. The journal is an instrument that will allow you to recall and revisit forgotten goals and dreams. Goals are an extension of your Human Worth. Without Human Worth, you may not be motivated to set goals because that would imply risking failure.

If your goal is to walk 3 days a week for 20 minutes each time, record the time you log or keep a diary. A written record not only shows how much progress you've made but also may help keep you on track when your motivation flags. Looking back at how far you've come makes you feel good about yourself. It also helps you develop a sense of self-efficacy, a belief in your own capabilities. When your sense of self-efficacy is high, you have the motivation to continue.[71]

You know yourself better than anyone else. You know best how to monitor your own progress. However, to stay on track we may need to bring others into the picture for encouragement. Starting new habits may call for a type of long-term support that mentors, close friends or family members can give. Listen to their input. They often have insights about your personality that others may not share. They can help by inspiring us, giving us knowledge and encouraging us to stay on the right track. However, *you* can also be one of your most effective sources of support and feedback. Celebrate and applaud yourself for your efforts. If you do a good job, don't say that anyone could have done as well—to do so would be to reject or discount your positive experience. Discounting the positive takes the joy out of life and makes you feel inadequate and unrewarded. Give yourself credit for everything you try to do.

"Happiness is not something ready-made. It comes from your own actions."
~ Dalai Lama

If you don't feel like you've made any progress, simply note what happened (without guilt or blame) in your journal and begin again. Starting over does not mean failure. Even when we don't get the results we want, we learn something valuable in the process.

---

[71] JoAnn Dahklloetter, *Your Performing Edge: The complete Mind-Body Guide for Excellence in Sports, Health and Life* (Carlos, CA: Pulgas Ridge Press, 2004).

With each goal achieved, no matter how small, you will gain confidence and your Self-Esteem will be increased.

Coping With Setbacks

"We make mistakes, mistakes don't make us"
~ Maxwell Maltz (1899-1975), surgeon, author

Did you know that Walt Disney was fired from a newspaper for lacking ideas? And that he also went bankrupt several times before he built Disneyland?

That Thomas Edison was thrown out of school in the early grades when his teacher decided he couldn't do the work?

That Michael Jordan barely made his high school varsity team because he was underweight and short?

These famously successful people all struggled with setbacks, but they were persistent and persevered in achieving their goals and dreams.

All human beings have one thing in common which is the struggle to survive. We all have an inner battleground where the forces of discouragement and the forces of determination constantly clash. Setbacks create feelings of discomfort and disappointment with ourselves, but don't let a moment of weakness derail your efforts. Slip-ups are almost inevitable. Self-resiliency is overcoming the seemingly impossible odds by bouncing back, moving forward, withstanding hardships, and getting on with our lives. "[Self-Resilience] is the ability to recover and effectively adjust to change or misfortunes. It refers to our ability to effectively deal with and optimally adjust to challenges and stress."[72] Self-resiliency is when you get slammed down to the ground but have the ability to get up and return to the fight. It means we can soar, move, advance, or climb above our difficulties in life.

It's a challenge to break old habits and develop new ones, and it's wise not to expect perfection. Many of us begin every new year with a list of worthy resolutions on which we follow through for a short while. Despite the attempt, most of us end up slipping back into our old habits. Making changes to our life isn't easy.

Revisiting your resolutions or goals plays a significant role in developing new habits. Are your goals crystal clear and specific? We've talked about this before; for example, how do you follow through on this vague goal: "I want to lose weight"? Instead, state

---

[72] Talia Ziv, Relational Resilience Coaching, http://www.drtaliaziv.com/7.html. Accessed Mar 2011.

the goal more specifically, "Go to the gym 3 times a week," leaving no room for misinterpretation.

Stay inspired. Visualize the new you. Start practicing self-affirming, positive thoughts to develop a more positive self-image. One suggestion is to find a picture of yourself when you looked fit and great—then, post it where you will see it every day. Don't use a photo of some lean athlete—that's not keeping it real, and you'll just get frustrated.

Keeping yourself motivated is another step towards achieving goals. Scale down your goal if it is too large or too time-consuming. Shrink down your efforts into more bite-size portions. Completion of the smaller goals will be rewarding achievements and keep you motivated to continue. Most people would agree that it is much more rewarding to travel around the globe if you stop in different countries along the way and spend time enjoying the different sights, peoples, foods, etc. than if you merely flew non-stop around the world.

Another way to cope with setbacks is to surround yourself with people and places that support your desire to change. Do not be a victim of your past or present. Stay away from negative people who will hinder the positive changes you want in your life. Socialize only with positive individuals. Seek out people who are supportive and can possibly also serve as mentors. If this is difficult, find people and organizations that give your life meaning and purpose.

When confronted with life's challenges, obstacles and adversities, you must trust the process of change. If you do slip back into your old habits or conditioned behaviors, avoid any self-judgment. Believe in your ability! Allow whatever time it takes to get back on track and make the changes you truly desire. For example, if you skipped your workout today and ate more than you wanted to at lunch, just make the necessary adjustments and get back on track. Be resilient and simply vow to try again. Research shows that how you respond to your setbacks is vital to your success—and a sign of your commitment to change.

My Own Physical Setbacks

Physical fitness was as much a part of my life as eating, sleeping or breathing. For many years, like a lot of other people, I took my health for granted. After all, I was a former athlete and training for football kept me active, my heart healthy and me in reasonably good shape. I was a relatively healthy child, so illness was foreign to me.

In February, 2000, the unexpected occurred. I had severe pain in my lower right side, nausea, vomiting, diarrhea, chills and fever. During a 10-day span, I was misdiagnosed by emergency room doctors three times, and there was no relief in sight from the pain. I was finally diagnosed with acute appendicitis and had to undergo emergency surgery. This was the first time in 36 years that I had a life-threatening health problem. My white blood count was over 30,000, and my condition was further complicated because it was discovered that my appendix had ruptured. The poison went out into my body causing major complications. The body I thought was a fortress for so many years had suddenly grown toxic and turned on me. The doctor explained the risks of having the surgery, and I felt I was caught between the devil and the deep blue sea. I had dreams to pursue, challenges to conquer, a story to tell, and a wife who loved and needed me.

Prior to my hospital admission, I knew intuitively that something was wrong with me; however I thought it would simply go away. I blamed my condition on not eating right or my not getting enough sleep and not exercising on a regular basis. I had simply lost the motivation to exercise because I was a workaholic. Exercising is like going to church; when you go regularly, it becomes a part of your life; when you stop, it is hard to motivate yourself to get back into it. It becomes easier to make excuses for not doing it.

My encounter with acute appendicitis accomplished two things: First, I realized that I had grown too comfortable in my life and stopped taking care of myself. Although I had lost my desire to exercise, the many years that I did paid off: The doctor stated that anyone else in my condition would have died and attributed my survival to my physical fitness. I was mortal after all and was suddenly forced to face the possibility of dying. Second, it introduced me to dependency on others. I was discharged from the hospital with an open wound from the surgery, but it then became infected. Nurses came to my home, and I was as helpless as a newborn baby; I had to depend on others for all of my basic needs. The illness drained my strength, and I had no energy left. It was the biggest physical setback I had ever experienced.

I cost the insurance company $44,633.13 for a 14-day hospital stay followed by several weeks of recuperating at home. Suddenly, all of the things that seemed more important in my life than taking care of myself were not quite as important any more. I knew that I was being given a second chance to accomplish my dreams and aspirations.

For a brief period of time, my illness was controlling who I was. Instead of trying to regain my strength and speed the healing process, I felt sorry for myself. I sank deeper and deeper into the darkness. I had forgotten the role that the mind and spirit plays in life. I allowed my worries, stress and the lack of exercise to steal the strength I needed to fight my illness. In a matter of months, my weight ballooned from 210 pounds to 280 pounds. Instead of being resilient and bouncing back, I failed to learn despite my brush with death.

I had forgotten that a positive outlook does wonders for the soul and the body. A positive outlook allows us to view things in their proper perspective without allowing them to alter our future. Thankfully, I began to recall my old attitude about life. I realized that hopefulness and hopelessness could not occupy the same space. I had a choice to make. Was I going to continue feeling hopeless or was I going to take the bull by the horns and regain control of both my body and my life?

Coming face to face with my own mortality was a very important experience for me. It showed me that I am not invincible and that I must take responsibility for my body. I can choose to remain healthy by taking a few moments out of each day to help myself or I can ignore my body and become another health statistic. The choice is mine, and the same choice is yours.

Today, I accept illness as a condition, but I refuse to accept it as a definition of who I am. Each of our roads to personal freedom begins with an understanding that we can rise above our adversities. Part of this freedom is the freedom to make good choices and change our lives for the better. We can keep replaying the movies of our past, or we can change the channel and choose a picture of a better life. The act of choosing a positive future is the first step to a brighter, more fulfilling future.

When I was a community organizer, I faced many challenges and adversities that tested my self-resiliency each and every day of the week—I was forced to deal with rejections, disappointments, and my own inadequacies. It was hard work and I struggled, but I never lost hope. I felt the fear but did it anyhow.

How do I continue to find the will to persevere and remain driven? Firstly, I have a firm belief that I can accomplish my tasks even when people tell me I can't and it's all because I rely on my worth and have learned to be confident and to respect and love myself unconditionally. I am driven by trust and belief in my worth. Fueled by passion and inner strength, I become strong, determined and persistent. If you do something long enough and hard enough, you can persevere and stay with it to the end.

Secondly, I also rely on others who have the skills, knowledge or credentials to help me achieve my goals. I build relationships and stay in communication with them as they help me impact the quality of life for others. They are a significant and sometimes critical source, not only of support and funding for community services and events, but, much more importantly, of encouragement and knowledge.

People in my community often struggle with undue hardships—often caused by their own socially unacceptable behaviors. They don't have solutions to their problems so they become fearful, angry, hurt, disappointed, and rejected. With little resources or support, they attempt to cope by screaming, fighting, hustling, and scheming. Many social conditions have restricted their ability to overcome the numerous negative influences in their environment—drugs, violence, physical and verbal abuse, poverty, lack of family structure or positive role models, hunger, exploitation, limited employment opportunities, etc. They are not resilient enough to overcome them; faced with adversity, they struggle and lose hope.

Some people do their best work when faced with a difficult situation or a major setback. How do they do this? Their Human Worth allows them to turn adversity into advantage with amazing confidence and faith. Human Worth is our survival mechanism to turn challenges into triumphs. People can be inspired by challenge. Challenges provide us with the best opportunity to grow strong and survive. Many of us are the victims of dysfunctional families. We cannot change our past, but we can change the way we understand it. We must stop dwelling in the past and blaming everyone but ourselves for our undesirable traits. We must renew our thinking, discard horrible memories and old habits, view ourselves in a more positive image, and choose or learn new routines that let us bounce back from any hurtful feelings.

We cannot totally eliminate inadequate or negative behaviors, but we must remove the control these negative tendencies have on our lives. The task is to learn and develop new ways of identifying, understanding and coping with the more negative behaviors in ourselves and to firmly believe in one's inner strength and worth. By using newly developed belief systems, we are able to connect to our sense of worth and overcome adversity.

Unfortunately, not every at-risk youth can be salvaged. Some will simply not believe in the power of their Human Worth, that their inherent worth can sustain them and provide the resiliency needed to bounce back and recover from hard times, setbacks or obstacles. The critical lack of Self-Esteem, Self-Dignity and Self-Worth explains why they behave negatively and why the cycles of abuse are too often passed from one generation to the next. However, there is always the hope that at some time in their lives, these troubled youth may become more open to the power of their Human Worth.

Choosing the right words and giving/receiving positive self-talk is a key to self-resiliency and overcoming setbacks. When I was a child, at least 9 times out of 10, I was told something negative about myself. Only 10% of the time did I hear positive talk. Positive thoughts about yourself and others tend to create positive outcomes. How we talk to ourselves affects our confidence and esteem. I have since learned how positive self-talk creates a lasting feeling of worth which allows you to confront, convert or replace old negative habits and beliefs with positive ones which bolster our resiliency at overcoming setbacks which can delay the fulfillment of our dreams and desires.

We are human beings constantly learning and growing in an ever-changing world. We can't undo the hurt already experienced. It can be a long and rocky road to recover from past pain. However, if you are determined, then nothing is impossible. You have to learn to go within yourself, become aware of your feelings, thoughts and deeds and then accept them. The next time you encounter a challenging situation, give yourself a kind of "self-talk" to move you in a good and positive direction. Tell yourself that your life has value, importance, meaning, and purpose and that you love yourself unconditionally. No matter what it takes to recover from your setbacks, keep going; in time, you will discover that you can overcome the challenges which inevitably will come your way. Give fresh commands to your internal monitor that you are whole and perfect. Learn to become self-assertive. Give yourself the freedom to say "yes" to healthy choices and "no" to unhealthy ones. Think "outside the box" of traditional learning and change your heart, draw out your humanity and stay happy and hopeful. One day, you will find that you can effectively adjust to the misfortunes and challenges in your life. Even the smallest of your victories and successes can reinforce your worth and enable you to make the positive changes you need to be happy. Your Human Worth gives you the power and freedom to succeed.

Vision

"Nothing happens unless first a dream..."
~ Carl Sandburg (1878-1967), American poet,
historian, novelist, folklorist

By definition, a vision is unclear and grand. A vision is not something you have, but it's something that has you. It is the fuel that drives you and gives direction to your life. It powers your dreams and puts you in control of your destiny. It uses the power of your imagination. It can inspire you. To have a vision is to look farther than your eye can see or your mind can dream, to rise above the low planes of mediocrity, to achieve greatness and to realize your hopes, goals and dreams. Visualizing is seeing something more clearly, helping our goals seem more possible and increasing our motivation to go in the right direction. A vision serves as an inspiration for you to commit, with passion and drive, to a goal or dream.

Corporations, institutions and companies publicize their visions. Vision statements are intended to influence management and staff to stay on track with the company's mission. They inspire, motivate and guide them into making the company grow strong, become the most successful entity it can be, maximize profits or, as in the case of some non-profits, to accomplish a good cause.

Our visions are how we see ourselves. We can set goals all day long, but if we cannot truly see ourselves achieving them, our goals will never be realized. To accomplish a goal, you must truly expect to achieve it which implies you have hope in bringing it about—and that, simply put, is having a vision. When you visualize, see your dreams and goals as if they were happening right now. See and feel yourself as though you've already crossed the finish line!

A vision is a great starting place for making changes in your lives. It is an articulation of your Human Worth and the image of what you want your future to look like. It's thinking "outside the box." It's when you engage your heart, mind and soul and attempt to visualize your possibilities. It's the mental picture of how you want your life to be, the future to which you want to commit. Having a vision shapes your perception and behavior.

"How will you get THERE if you don't know where you're going?"

A vision gets you "there"—the "there" is the how, where and what you want to be. It reminds me of the story about the three men who were excited about getting to an island in the Caribbean. The first man decided to travel by plane because it was the fastest and most expedient way to get "there." The second man decided to travel by boat because it was the most relaxing and most scenic way of getting "there." The third man decided to travel by canoe which was the most difficult and painful way to get "there." The one thing they all had in common was the "there"—because there is a "there."

And so it should be with our own entity—the Self. We need a vision to get us THERE....the "there" being wherever it is you want to go or whatever it is that you want to accomplish in your life's journey.

<u>Visions of a Better Life</u>

My college years were a significant time in my life. My first year at Southern University can only be described as a learning experience. I was a young man away from my home environment for the first time in my life. I had been abused, bullied, labeled dysfunctional, and struggled within a violent socio-economic environment. I was now free to make my own decisions. I was on top of the world because I became a football star familiar to the screams of thousands of cheering fans. I felt like my life had meaning and purpose. My past was becoming a distant fading memory, and I had a new future. The only problem was that I had no earthly idea of how to create that future and I quickly learned that, on some occasions, I had not made the wisest choices.

My college experiences showed me that I could have a better life for myself. I did not know when I stepped onto the campus of Southern University that God had a plan for me and that my life was about to change. It was not until I entered my second year that I was given a glimpse of what a good life could be like. It was my first opportunity to witness the bonds of love and the inner workings of what psychologists term a "functional family." At times, it seemed like I had stepped into the pages of a fairytale.

My roommate that year was named Lance Hughes. Lance was born and bred in Baton Rouge and was the youngest of four children. He was a gifted physical education major and lived on campus. His father, Samuel Hughes and only sister, Karen, were educators in the Baton Rouge Public School System.

Lance Hughes & James Evans
at Southern University's photo day

120

His mother, Yvonne Hughes, was the supervisor of housing on the college campus. His oldest brother, Patrick, was a banker and his other brother, Daryl, was a professor at the college. At the time, we had no idea that his family was going to become an example to me of what life could be like...and that his family was to become my family.

The Hughes family was the most unique group of people I had ever encountered during my young life. Their extended family included grandparents and a stranger who just happened to be me. They demonstrated how life could be rather than how my life had been. I knew instantly that I wanted this type of life for myself. Ironically, there were times when I wished my own family could have witnessed how other people lived. However, it was not something I could share with the people back home.

The Hughes family was not wealthy by any stretch of the imagination. They were goal-oriented, they understood the need for a solid education and they knew that dreams were possible as long as you possessed an education, determination, inspiration, and ambition. During the years I spent with them, I never once saw them argue. They taught me that it was okay to agree to disagree with each other without hanging on to anger. They focused on loving and understanding each other.

The Hughes Family & Grandchildren

After Lance and I became roommates, I learned how to truly live the college experience. We enjoyed all of the things that college students usually enjoyed; however, we also realized that the family had a zero tolerance for not giving your best in the classroom. Therefore, obtaining a college education, which was the primary purpose of being there, was the only option.

The Hughes Family was Catholic, and I often attended mass with them, followed by a family dinner. Mr. Hughes loved dogs and fishing and enjoyed his hobbies immensely. He also took an interest in my football career, and we talked about each game I played afterwards.

In essence, Mr. Hughes became the father that was missing from my life. He helped fill the empty void that haunted me for so many years. I am not sure if he ever really realized the impact he had on my life or that he became my role model. In fact, I don't think he even saw himself in that role. He was just doing what came naturally to him, assuming the role of leader, teacher, friend, confidante, and protector. He was the epitome of what a man should be, and it seemed effortless on his part. Now, as a grown man myself, I realize that there had to have been times in his life when things were hard for him. Instead of drawing himself into a tight ball and hiding from the world until the problems went away, he met them head on, like a warrior on the battlefield.

James & Mr. Hughes

Mrs. Hughes may not have realized her importance in my life either, but she played a vital role in teaching me that nothing was without a price. During the summers, she would hire Lance and me to scrub the floors of the dormitories. It was hard work, but she nurtured both of us as she shaped and molded us for the future roles we would have in life. She became the mother of my dreams.

As close to perfect as the Hughes family appeared to be, they were not immune to sadness, death or violence. Their son, Daryl, went to a bowling club in a less than perfect area of town in his new sporty car. Someone attempted to take his vehicle; he fought back and was murdered.

That incident made me realize that I was not dreaming and that this family was real and mortal. Although there were so many positive things going on in their lives, they were still capable of being touched by violence and tragedy. There was never any real closure because the perpetrator was never apprehended. The loss of Daryl was very hard on the family, but, in spite of this tragedy, their love for one another and for me was faultless.

The thing I did not understand was how to accept this unconditional love that I suddenly had the good fortune to encounter. I found myself holding my breath waiting for the other shoe to fall. I felt this type of life was just too good to be true. I did not know how to express my gratitude for what they gave me. They did not know the past I had left behind in Prichard, Alabama. They did not know about the times I went to bed hungry or that I made sure I didn't miss school because that was a guaranteed meal. They did not know of the hurt and pain I harbored from experiences I faced in my young life. They saw a young physically-fit student who earned a scholarship…and that scholarship brought me to their front door.

I have maintained close bonds with the Hughes family, occasionally returning to Baton Rouge for various special occasions. I will always be grateful to this family because they taught me so much in such a short time. They gave me a solid foundation to build upon and never asked for anything in return. They will always have a special place in my heart because I owe them a debt that I can never repay. I now know that God was in charge of my life even before I sought Him out. He placed me in the path of this family to observe a life different from anything I had ever experienced.

The Hughes family served as an inspiration for me; for the first time in my life, I could envision a better future for myself. I hope that my life will serve to help others whom I encounter along my life's journey and enable them to envision better lives for themselves.

By coaching others and encouraging their self-expression, mentors facilitate their personal growth. In high school, it was my coaches, George Walker and Joe Collins, who taught me to have goals and dream of a better future. They pushed me beyond what I perceived were my limitations. When others were telling me what I could not do, they told me what I could do. If they only knew how their words inspired me and my vision, they would learn how I got to be where I am today—teaching the power of Human Worth to all who seek, need or have lost sight of it.

In my college years, besides Mr. Hughes, it was my university instructors and my coaches, Otis Washington and Bob Bennett, who taught me to have a grand vision for my life. And so I started writing and aspired to make those visions a reality. They exposed me to ideas and ways of life that I embraced with excitement and anticipation. I envisioned my life to be more successful like theirs.

Vision is not a luxury but a necessity. A vision helps you make your goals and dreams a reality, but without it, you drift in confusion about your purpose. If you are not dreaming, then others will do it for you. How do you achieve your goals and dreams without knowing what they look like? One way to make your grand visions a reality is to write down, internalize and visualize specific goals and dreams which was discussed previously in the section "Taking Action."

To bring a vision to life requires you taking full responsibility for what you choose to believe (or not) and for what you choose to act on (or not). It requires being your own authority figure. With no one to turn to for approval or to rebel against, you and you alone are capable of and responsible for the planning, prioritizing and building of your dreams...Go for it!...Believe that your vision is possible!

Describe what you want to see for yourself in the future. What kind of changes are you willing to experience in your lifetime? When creating your vision, are you daring enough to take risks and aim high? Are you willing to fight with all of your might for your dreams? Human Worth helps us to do what others have told us time and time again we couldn't do. The limitations they placed on us were based on their own limited abilities—not ours. When it comes to our visions, we must stay positive, determined and resilient while at the same time staying open to constructive criticism and possible modifications to our visions. It is vital to have people around us who can share the wisdom and insight of their life experiences and teach us valuable lessons. A mentor is just such a person who has the ability to make our dreams and visions explode into reality.

A vision can serve as a self-fulfilling prophesy that will constantly motivate you and act as a road map directing you to your goals. Visualize an image of yourself one year from today; picture where you will be, how you will feel and what you will be doing. Try your best to picture what it will all be like. Stay motivated, move steadily forward with your vision and eventually your vision will become reality!

It's imperative that we embrace our Human Worth as we work on our vision. While a vision opens up your mind to opportunities and creative new ideas and expectations, it is your Human Worth and set of values that will keep the vision functioning, guide you and bridge the present to the future. Do not underestimate the power of your Human Worth; it is the key to manifest your visions. The more we practice its power, the more our vision will become a reality. It enables us to move forward with confidence. When it is at the core of our being, we can rely on it every day to impress our visions and dreams into our subconscious mind and fulfill those dreams and visions with belief and inspiration.

When your vision lacks the power of Human Worth you will struggle to set goals. You will find that by the end of a deadline they have not been achieved or are even forgotten. You may give-up, become bitter or slide back into old negative habits that limit your opportunities to get closer to your vision. Stay away from naysayers as you attempt to fulfill your hopes, goals and dreams. If and when you make "mistakes," think of them as lessons that warn you when you are going off course or when you will miss the "there." Learn from them, so you are constantly re-aligning yourself to your goals and dreams. Achieving your goals then becomes a reality instead of just a dream.

Ask yourself these questions: "What is the vision you have for your future?" "Has your vision been limited by your past failures, present fears or your uncertainty?" If you only have a vague answer to these questions, then you have never given yourself the freedom to dream. When you are in tune with your Human Worth, you are free to not only discover, but also to fulfill the desires of your heart.

Vision allows you to reach for what you really want. It causes you to see beyond the horizon of challenges and obstacles and into the future you desire. Everyone's vision is unique and incorporates one's beliefs and values; more importantly, it should speak to what makes you happy and joyful. Only then will it move you to fulfill your dreams. If you want to maximize your personal potential, you must have a vision inside you!

Vision is closely related to Hope. They are both key to unlocking the hidden and denied talents of our unfilled potential. Hope is an optimistic belief that a positive outcome lies ahead. Hope is a way of thinking, feeling and acting that helps us find ways to live with difficult situations. Hope is a wish, a feeling that what is wanted can be obtained—that what we want to occur is a possibility. It allows us to stay strong as we keep believing that things will turn out for the best or that our circumstances will change.

In my experience in working with others, I have learned that the underlying condition which makes us grasp for hope is a sense of desperation or dissatisfaction with life as it is. Too many people have lost sight of their Human Worth and are hopeless. Some believe their situations are without hope unless they have more money. They argue that without money they cannot envision success. There are people who, despite having loving husbands or wives and families, choose suicide, drugs and alcohol. If they would only understand the importance of their Human Worth and have hope, then their lives would turn out differently.

Sometimes, it's others who may tell them that their situation is hopeless; other times it may be that their hopes are unrealistic. This may make it more difficult to manage their current situation. We can't always change the outcome of a situation, but we can decide what part hope will play in dealing with the situation.

If you are struggling with your Worth, don't have a vision or your vision is eluding you, then it's easy to lose hope and suffer from despair. When people are deep in despair and anguish, hope seems unreachable. If you find yourself in need of hope, then repeat these words to yourself over and over again, "I love myself unconditionally, my life has meaning and purpose, my life has value and importance. I am confident in who I am." Do not let adversity dim your hope. Hope will allow you to cope with the difficult situations in your life.

Hope tends to provide a sort of fantasy or escape route which allows us to hold ourselves at arm's length from our pain and discomfort in the hope that tomorrow will be better. The "Cinderella complex" is a good example of a hope-based fantasy— that someday a prince will somehow show up on a white stallion, sweep poor little Cinderella off her feet and save her from her miserable little life and suffering. Even when things about your future seem discouraging, you can choose how you will face these challenges. There's always hope! Never let go of hope. One day, you will see that it all has finally come together. What you have always wished for will finally come to be and you have finally arrived at your "there." When you look back at your progress, you may even laugh at how it all came about.

Vision and hope are just doorways to the other side—to our future—but we must *act* on our hopes and visions. Vision gives us direction on how to pursue whatever gives our lives meaning and purpose and then catapults us into action. Hope gives us the belief that what we want in life is possible. As we travel in our journey through the process of self-discovery and self-realization, all the various systems of the body working together will give us the energy and drive to begin realizing our vision. Everything about us will function in harmony, and we will experience a personal transformation into the life God designed for us.

Embrace Change and Be Free at Last!

"All of us should strive for a newer and better self—take our lives to the next level" ~ LL Cool J[73]

Think about it for a moment. If you're going through any challenges right now, this can be just the moment when the tide can turn your way—and away from disruptive and unhealthy conditioned behaviors and emotions. Choosing to make positive life changes, even with a very small step, can be a comeback time for you. What may have once seemed to be a breakdown can now be a breakthrough. Make your challenges a time of resurrection, renewal, restoration, rebirth, and return to your true Self.

Any actions we complete to transform our lives can liberate us and enable us to overcome our perceived limitations. With the appropriate changes and the adoption of constructive behavior patterns, we will grow personally, socially and emotionally. We will gain a new sense of order and purpose in life. Change itself is a mood-enhancer and makes us feel happier; we relax, improve our mental health and have more energy to channel into desirable activities. Success in our personal and work lives will increase. We will "get on" with our lives with a minimum of delay or confusion, which previously resulted in avoidance of change. We will identify new strengths and resources perhaps not evident earlier.

What Changed My Life/Letting Go

While I was in the NFL, I received major recognition for a motivational speech that I gave to a group of youths in public school. My "ABC's of Confident Thinking" speech was so inspiring and moving that, when the video tape of it was brought to the media, it drew national attention. And thus did my journey begin. I felt proud of myself and feelings of happiness stirred within me. Looking into the eyes of those young people inspired me in ways I could not have foreseen and was one of the reasons I started the Tampa Bay Academy of Hope. I began to educate and motivate myself to find out about my Human Worth. I became obsessed with wanting to read and write more about self-worth. I learned how to become self-confident, have self-respect, be self-determined, and to really "meet myself for the very first time."[74] I learned how necessary it was to let go of issues from my past in order to come to a full acceptance and acknowledgment of who I really am. This

---

[73] American rapper/singer, actor in a *Parade magazine* article, "Sarcasm is the Key to Our Bonding," 17 Jan 2010, p 5.
[74] A reference to the title of my autobiography, my first self-published book.

has allowed me to take control of my life. Passionate and motivated, I became driven by a vision to inspire and uplift others about my newly found Human Worth.

For many years, I internalized a sense of inadequacy and was unable to fully love and accept myself. I struggled with anxious feelings of emptiness and insufficiency which I fought to fill up with work, achievement and status. I hadn't yet learned that, until I embraced every aspect of my real Self with genuine love and compassion, no amount of success would lead to my happiness and no relationship would ever be good enough. My inner happiness does not come from my wife, family or friends, but from a mature self-acceptance, self-esteem, self-confidence, and an unconditional love of my Self.

In my life's journey to learn about the power of Human Worth, I learned that when I choose to take responsibility for my feelings, I am free from the control of others. It seemed that sooner or later everyone I knew would eventually disappoint me. They would say or do something that would hurt or anger me. A rude remark or an insensitive action from others is inevitable. But, empowered with self-worth, I learned not to feel threatened when they were having a bad day. I discovered that the key to establishing a healthy, lasting relationship is to stop trying to control someone else's behavior, choices or feelings. I learned that I cannot give real, unconditional love as long as I let their hurtful words and actions adversely affect my love for them. As long as I blamed others for my feelings, I was stuck. I was the helpless victim.

There is great freedom in conquering rejection or disapproval. I have empowered myself to forgive those who have hurt me because I understand that letting go is the most rewarding feeling one can have. In letting go, you ultimately free yourself from bondage. My life is richer and fuller since I decided to let go of past regrets and embark on the journey of finding my true Self, acknowledging my Human Worth and making changes in my life to become the happiest and most fulfilled person I can be.

"When I let go of what I am, I become what I might be." ~ Lao Tzu

Making conscious decisions to value your worth and take responsibility for your thoughts and actions can give you personal power. We need to learn to overcome our fears about change. Using our power we can conquer the fears and conditioned behaviors which once made us servants to their demands. Keep this ubiquitous quotation in mind whenever obstacles come your way: *"Life isn't about waiting for the storm to pass...It's about learning to dance in the rain."*

I want to share with you an especially powerful, poignant and inspirational video on the YouTube website that is dear to my heart. It's of one of my very own former TBAH students, Winsome

Jackson, as she gave her stirring and emotional speech, "Who Am I?" at the TBAH's Annual Banquet in June, 2008. This is a "must see," and I urge you to view it online at:

http://www.youtube.com/watch?v=qjN_RIHfpEA&feature=channel.

For those of you who do not have internet access, Winsome tells a stirring and compelling story of how after coming to the Academy she overcame seemingly insurmountable obstacles and made major changes in her life. Winsome was the first in her family to graduate high school; she then went on to attend Florida State University where she planned to major in law.

Embracing change gives you the freedom to do what needs to be done to make your life the way you would like it to be. By adjusting successfully to change, you will be free to reap the benefits of your human potential. Great causes are not accomplished overnight. Changing yourself takes time and commitment. The changes you make that connect you to your Human Worth will point you in the right direction in your life's journey. Never underestimate yourself, work towards your goal, take small steps, enjoy the journey, and you WILL get there.

"It's never too late to be who you might have been."
~ George Eliot *(1819—1880), English novelist*

One of the reasons I founded the Tampa Bay Academy of Hope was to help at-risk youths and their parents to make meaningful changes in their lives and empower them to rise above the numerous adversities and challenges they faced every day. Day in and day out, it amazed me to see them gain control of their negative belief systems, change their behaviors and become more aware of their inner strengths and worth.

MY LEGACY: THE TAMPA BAY ACADEMY OF HOPE

"Each one of us has the choice to use the gift of our lives to make the world a better place."
　　　　　~ Dr. Jane Goodall, English scientist (primate behavior), author[75]

I understand that I am standing on the shoulders of those who made me feel like I mattered and now the question is "What will *I* leave behind for the next generation?" No one can survive living simply from moment to moment, denying the future. There has to be a rhythm and connection to something bigger. My life's experiences have given me the wisdom to find the courage to take action to touch the lives of others. A willingness to care enough to take action and make a difference is what leaving a legacy is all about.

The idea of leaving something behind that will "live forever" is appealing. We want to feel like we matter in the vast sea of humanity. Legacy may remind us of death, but it's not about death. A legacy is really about life and living. It helps us to decide the kind of life we want to live and the kind of world we want to live in. Without working to create a legacy, people can lose meaning in their life. A legacy may take many forms: children, grandchildren, a business, an ideal, a book, a community, a home, or some piece of ourselves. From a purely practical standpoint, if you don't pass on your life experience by leaving a legacy, the wisdom you've gained through decades of learning will disappear as your physical body wears out. When you have passed from this life and you are missed, that is a measure of your true Human Worth.

---

[75] Pant Hoot quarterly newsletter, Issue I, Winter 2006. www.janegoodall.org.

"We realize that what we are accomplishing is a drop in the ocean. But if this drop were not in the ocean, it would be missed."
~ Mother Theresa

When thinking about the icons who influenced my life—the coaches who encouraged me, the Mother Teresa's and Gandhi's whose lives inspired me and built up my sense of Self-Worth—I often wondered and asked myself, "How can I have the kind of impact that makes a lasting difference in the lives of others?" Their messages and life stories were so powerful to me that, after my short career in professional football, I wanted to do what others did for me. I felt that the essential purpose of my life was to serve others. I also wanted to make a difference. I wanted to reverse the cycle of poverty for troubled and under-privileged youths in our communities. Therefore, I made the selfless decision to go back into my community to increase awareness about the importance of Human-Worth and emphasize the value of education. I decided to mentor troubled youths who lacked encouragement and guidance from positive role models or mentors.

In July, 1996, empowered by my Human Worth and armed with confidence, determination and pride, I took a huge risk and founded a non-profit organization, the Tampa Bay Academy of Hope, Inc.(TBAH), and became its Executive Director. My mission was to strengthen youth development in lower-income communities and work with struggling, inner-city youth and their parents. For the first two years, I funded TBAH with my own money and also seed money from sponsors and fund-raising activities. Initial seed money came from G. H. Johnson Construction Co., (now Johnson Cutler) and the Life Skills Foundation, who hired me as a consultant, thus enabling me to fund and incorporate as a non-profit organization. TBAH provided comprehensive programs whereby youth successfully made the transition from a life of hopelessness, poverty and dependency to one of leadership, prosperity and independence.

I designed a leadership-through-education model that has fostered worth, love, self-esteem, self-resiliency and has given value, importance, purpose, and meaning to the lives of disadvantaged youth and their parents who have lost sight of their worth. This model changes lives and enables others to do the same in their communities and organizations. Its programs focused on enabling youths and their parents to find the inner strength to overcome their fears and hopelessness and connect to their Human Worth.

At the Academy, most of my students were unaware of or insensitive to their negative ingrained behaviors. To address and overcome them, they were taught to examine their history to discover the root of many of their problems. They were provided with role models, books, activities, and programs that helped them to identify, understand and cope with the negative tendencies and self-fulfilling prophesies that impacted their lives. They were taught how to be resilient and how to develop the confidence to gain control of their behaviors and adjust to life's challenges and stress. They were taught that they can break the generational cycle by developing a new system of thinking: to deal creatively with the past, present and future possibilities they had to cultivate their strengths. By doing this, they obtained the courage to test their limits, manage their anger, overcome their hurt, and bear their grief with assurance and conviction. By changing their self-talk, troubled youths can stop being the victim. They learn to choose the right words to encourage themselves, such as, "I don't have to be like my mother or father," "I don't have to drink, smoke or use violence," or "I choose to stop dwelling in the past and the hurt that I have suffered." When they got slammed down to the ground, I taught them to bounce back.

Story of D'Andre, 17 years old, high school graduate 2000

"I grew up in search of a sense of belonging and in need of love...I felt all alone with no one in my corner, living from day to day wondering how I [was] going to make it....[In the] summer of 1997, at a critical point in my life, I wanted to commit suicide and leave this world behind. At this point; I was dealing with a life of hopelessness, loneliness, worthlessness, rejection, and despair. I was hurting; life had lost it meaning and purpose for me as a young man.

That's when I was referred to an organization called the Tampa Bay Academy of Hope. I called to set up a time to go and meet with the program's director, that's when I heard the words "You're someone special at the Tampa Bay Academy of Hope. How can I help you?" Right then and there, I felt like I could give life a second chance. [He] presented himself to me with unconditional love that did not judge who I was, where I've been, and where I was going. And I knew that I had come to the right place that summer.

"Papa Bear," also known as Mr. Evans, along with others gave me the opportunity and the tools to take life on and have a second chance at becoming a man. Papa Bear and Mama Bear, also known as Mrs. Gail, took me into their home, provided me with transportation, helped me return to school at Hillsborough Community College and gain employment at JP Morgan Chase. I opened a bank account, joined a local church and changed my life forever....[I] stand as testimony that a life can be changed with love, hope and education.

The Tampa Bay Academy of Hope keeps it real!!! Even though I made a lot of mistakes they never gave up on me…even through the death of my mother and my plans not going the way I intended. I can remember the lessons of love and hope that was given to me at The Tampa Bay Academy of Hope. I will always be forever grateful for the commitment and dedication of men and women who sacrificed their time, talents, and their treasures to give me a second chance in life."

D'Andre attended Hillsborough (Tampa) Community College, became a manager of a furniture store in Atlanta, Ga., and now works in manufacturing.

August, 2011—D'Andre's wedding in Georgia
Me, on left, as Best Man

Many years ago, as D'Andre was overcoming his adversities, he felt that I had so impacted his life that he vowed to have me as his best man if and when he ever got married. As his mentor, I had saved and changed this young man's life who managed to triumph over his setbacks and move on with his life. In August, 2011, at D'Andre's invitation, I attended his wedding as best man and also served to "stand in" for his deceased father. I had again done what my mentors had done for me.

TBAH was created because I realized that I could not separate myself from or shed my past, but I could use those life experiences to give hope to others. I am convinced that all people's lives have meaning and purpose, but my passion was, and still is, with disadvantaged and troubled youths with whom I could identify—those who were trapped from birth in social and economic situations and circumstances that made them feel worthless. These troubled youths believe they're not "smart" enough, they're not "light" enough or they don't live in the "right" neighborhood. Their sense of worth is so compromised that they behave in ways that society has deemed inadequate and unacceptable. Anger and violence are their prerequisite for resolving issues. They do not embrace their Human Worth birthright—their place in God's universe. They believe that this is the hand that life has dealt them. They are left to flounder.

Story of Tamyla, 17 years old, high school graduate 2009

".. At the time I'm writing this essay my mother is incarcerated. So, my nineteen year-old sister is providing for my twelve year-old sister and me. My mother enrolled me into this program [ie, TBAH] in the beginning of my ninth grade year. I did not know what college was, nor did I have any clue of what I wanted to do after school.

With my situation, I don't think I would've even finished school without The Tampa Bay Academy of Hope. I always knew there was a future somewhere and was praying every night wishing days would get better. I thank God that a way has been made for me to become a successful young lady.

This program has made me think...[about my] future. Thanks to the Tampa Bay Academy of Hope, my mindset has changed in many ways; this program has helped me in school and outside of school. I plan to have many titles behind my name, to become the first woman to succeed at something no other woman has done in my family.

Once I am very successful, I will give back and help my peers, who are going through the same situation, to continue with life. I'll let them know your life doesn't end there; life is much more than you have experienced. You go through these things, because the outcome makes you successful.

I am very thankful for the Tampa Bay Academy of Hope."

Tamyla went on to attend Florida A&M University studying to become a doctor.[76]

It disturbed me to see that so many were not connected to their Human Worth. I witnessed their tears, fears and emotional turmoil. I felt their pain, hurt and feelings of worthlessness...and it made my heart heavy.

I am whole-heartedly adamant and passionate about doing my part to transform human worthlessness into human potential in our communities. There is no greater feeling on earth than to motivate and help others change their lives, to help them see the goodness, usefulness and importance in and of themselves and others—irrespective of their status or material wealth.

---

[76] This is another must see and you are urged to view it online at:
http://www.youtube.com/watch?v=3acTmbf4gNs&feature=relmfu. Tamyla tells a compelling story of how she became the first in her family to finish high school go on to Florida A&M University where she planned to be a doctor.

<u>Story of Monique, 17 years old, high school graduate 2009</u>

"If the Tampa Bay Academy of Hope was not here, it would be a great loss in my life as well as…the community as a whole. The Tampa Bay Academy of Hope has been a source of hope for kids who may not have even envisioned finishing high school, much less going to college.

With so many challenges facing us today, we need a place and people who encourage us to not only succeed, but to excel. Mr. Evans, Mr. Gainer and Mr. Gibson encourage me to reach higher. I'm reminded to use my God-given gifts to not only benefit myself but my community as well.

If the Tampa Bay Academy of Hope was not here, I would miss the opportunity of a lifetime to have firsthand exposure and knowledge of the local, state and federal legislative systems. The very fact that I worked to go on the trip has made this a valuable lesson for me. Oftentimes, if we are given things we don't appreciate them, but when we help earn our way it makes them more valuable and meaningful.

Without the Tampa Bay Academy of Hope, I may not have had the chance to go and see places and people. I can only thank God that the Tampa Bay Academy of Hope is here to offer hope, vision and victory to my generation. "

Monique went on to attend a Florida university.

My organization's mission statement was a powerful one: "To reverse the cycle of poverty, crime and educational underachievement in economically depressed areas by instilling leadership, responsibility and Self-Esteem in youth that will transition them from lives of hopelessness, poverty and dependency to self-sufficiency." The only thing left for me to do was to make it happen. However, before I could enforce the focus on education, I also had to convince them that they were worth it.

I knew the vicious generational cycle of poverty, crime and educational underachievement could not be broken from the outside. It could only be dismantled from the inside. They had to be able to see life from new perspectives; I had to lead them through a transformational process to change their old beliefs and ways of thinking and behaving.

I knew that judges, prosecuting attorneys, police officers, jailers, and even teachers could not understand these children because they could not relate to them. While the judges were preparing their families for summer vacations and outings, some of these children were shoplifting in order to eat. While the police officers were only concerned with the volume of paperwork an arrest produced, these children were fighting off drug dealers and rapists. While the teachers were only concerned about pushing them through the system, the children were wondering when they would be forced to move again because their family could not pay the rent. I understood these things because I had lived them.

Story of Brianna, 18 years old, high school graduate 2009

"If the Tampa Bay Academy of Hope were not around, I would be far from where I am now....For a short period, I rebelled against my mother, not because I didn't love her, but because I felt she didn't love me. One of the first things Hope helped me get over was that I needed to love myself.

They showed me that it wasn't my mother who didn't love me, it was I who didn't love myself. They showed me that I didn't need someone to tell me what I was or wasn't.

I was an angry person, so I would shut down around other people...This made me unfriendly and very closed-minded. The Tampa Bay Academy of Hope showed me that I had no reason to be angry with anyone for what happens in my life, because it was my life and everything I saw wrong in someone else was what I saw wrong in myself. TBAH taught me to have pride in myself...

If The Tampa Bay Academy of Hope were not a part of my life, I would not be the determined and motivated young woman that I am today...focused on my future."

Brianna went on to attend Argosy University.

The Academy provided intense mentoring and support to Hillsborough County's at-risk, underprivileged middle and high school students. Students were supported with tutoring and intense case management. We encouraged and taught them to take full responsibility for their behaviors or any decisions they made. "Hope," as the Academy was often affectionately referred to, gave these students the unique and specialized mentoring that helped them graduate high school and graduate into productive and fulfilling lives. With Hope, thousands of these youth graduated as professionals and community leaders and proved the program's success time after time.[77]

---

[77] The Academy still actively exists; however, the past tense is used to indicate that these efforts occurred before I retired from TBAH. Some highlights from the years of my leadership may be viewed at: http://www.youtube.com/watch?v=fUDEcn3_TrA&feature=related

A partnership with the Hillsborough County School District (HCSD), the 8th largest school district in the U.S., enabled TBAH to build a strong relationship with school officials who identified students in 10 middle and high schools in the Tampa area who were at risk of both criminal and disruptive behavior. The HCSD assigned these students to the Academy and helped to fund its programs that served 100-150 students from ages 12 to 18 per school year.

The students remained under the watchful supervision of TBAH for their entire middle and high school career and were prepared by the Academy to attend college. They were taken on various tours throughout the year: to colleges to expose them to the process of higher education and to circuit judges, legislators on the academy's Legislator Tour (from Tampa, to Tallahassee, and then Washington, D.C.) which allowed them to view government in action.[78] In 2010, we started the Tour of Justice where students have breakfast with judges from the 13th Circuit Court of Hillsborough County, Florida, followed by a tour of the judge's chambers and court rooms where they listened to cases and verdicts involving juveniles. They also met annually with a panel of leaders in the Juvenile Justice community. These kinds of close and up-front encounters with people from colleges and the outside community helped to widen the social and educational horizons and opportunities of these disadvantaged youth.

Story of Dontae, 18 years old, high school graduate 2009

"...nothing I have experienced or learned in any of...[my other] programs compares to what I have encountered in my time with Tampa Bay Academy of Hope. My club sponsor about a year ago first told me about Hope, she was very enthusiastic about the program and wanted me to get involved almost immediately. One thing that really pulled me into the idea was that this organization was Christian-based, something that was absent from my other programs. I went to the first meeting and actually had the opportunity to talk with my sponsors who were successful, well-respected African American males, which was a first for me. I also noticed the kind of relationship that existed between them and other kids. It was so structured, yet there was a family atmosphere. Since then, there has not been one meeting with them where I have not taken something back with me that will only better me in the future.

---

[78] To view highlights of the 2008 legislative tour visit:
http://www.youtube.com/watch?v=fUDEcn3_TrA&feature=related.

Now to even fathom the idea of such an organization not being in existence is something I find almost completely impossible. The non-existence of this program would not only distort our view on our goals and how to achieve them, but it would take away the faces of the type of people whom we associate with success and whom we label with the title of "role model."

The Tampa Bay Academy of Hope and all of the people involved have taught us how to prepare for our future in the best way possible. Some kids who have been a part of Hope since their seventh grade year have been exposed to so much and to never have had that could mean nothing but lost potential. Not having a good foundation of support, especially for those in my generation, is something this society cannot afford. Being able to have some place to go after school, to do something academically productive and also be surrounded by individuals who understand and are there for you is something that you cannot get just anywhere.

Personally, I believe the one thing that would be missing if Hope did not exist would be awareness of [the] fact that there are Black men in high places doing positive life-changing things with our generation. Especially in a society that through media, entertainment and everyday life depict the African-American male as a subject who is underachieved, disadvantaged and not worth the effort. The absence of them would psychologically lead us (meaning other young black males), to believe that taking on such roles of leadership are not within our grasp.

In essence, the absence of this organization would not only leave a void but would perpetuate the negative, hopeless views that plague our black youth today."

Dontae went on to attend Florida A&M University majoring in Mass Communications.

When the kids beat themselves down, TBAH picked them up with Hope. It provided coaches, father figures, role models, etc. who served as mentors inspiring the youth to believe that there was Hope. Our mentors provided them with hands-on experiences and took part in the education of their character. They helped them to explore careers and to gain access to online educational resources (including tutorial websites, testing/college admissions information and Hillsborough County Public Schools' online resources). They also helped them to prepare in the reading, writing, math, and science areas of the annual FCATs (Florida Comprehensive Assessment Tests, administered to grades 3-11).

Despite the fact that 98% of its participants continued on to college, the non-profit always struggled with funding and insufficient personnel. Although the Academy learned how to do much with very little, these perennial issues always plagued the organization. Contributions were always much needed to fund the programs and services that the Academy provided. Without external financial support, TBAH could not have lasted for the 15 years under my direction.

The mission of TBAH was accomplished through a four-step approach in a Leadership Through Education model. (See Appendix B for a detailed description of this model.) TBAH also developed a system of recognizing the achievements of program participants. In partnership with the Boy Scouts of America, each young person was awarded merit badges and stipends based on their successful participation in the program. In addition, they were honored in a celebration at the end of each school year.

Starting in 1999, the TBAH conducted an annual three-day leadership conference called the "Skills of Hope Youth Leadership Conference." This event allowed youngsters to participate and engage in leadership development workshops, culminating in a banquet that celebrated positive Self-Esteem. As a result of the success of these conferences, other workshops were added in 2001 and 2002, and the conference continued to grow. The following excerpted newspaper article explains the details:[79]

"...The theme for this year's Skills Of Hope Youth Leadership Conference is 'Focusing on the Strengths of our Youths.' Several area businesses and agencies have contributed to the success of this conference. Each year some 118 corporations volunteer their services.

...Evening activities will be highlighted with a concert for the youth and the community. Following the concert, the youngsters will get to know each other.

Saturday, following breakfast, is filled with a number of workshops-on "Leadership" ..."Successful Interviewing" ... "Managing Anger/Self-Esteem" ... "Hygiene/Etiquette" [and] "Abstinence." The youngsters will also participate in a rap session... A panel of physicians will conduct a workshop on "It's About Life." Saturday evening, the middle school and high school students will be treated to a Self-Esteem Dinner and Talent Show.

On Sunday, the role of the parents will be explored through workshops..."That's the unique part about this conference," states James Evans, founder. "Parents must have a role in the lives of their children."...While the parents are in workshops, the youngsters will be entertained at Busch Gardens.

...Evans said, "...it's very critical to find young individuals who have the desire to impact other peoples' lives as leaders." From the 200 who attend, 50 will be

---

[79] Gwendolyn Hayes, "200 Youth To Benefit From Youth Leadership Conference," *The Florida Sentinel,* 13 Sept 2002.

selected to participate in a 12-month program...Parents are also required to participate during the 12 months. "When the parents are involved you produce effective and strong leaders; you teach them how to be balanced in our community, which goes along with our motto of giving, becoming, knowing and belonging."

I am proud to say that the TBAH will become a part of my legacy. But the Academy's youth are themselves a part of this legacy as another local newspaper article pointed out. [80]

"He is the creator of the "Skills of Hope Youth Leadership Conference," held annually in Tampa, Florida. The conference, begun in 2001, teaches leadership through education, and shows youth how to take responsibility for their lives, family, education, and community. A highlight of the conference is a formal Self-Esteem Banquet where youth showcase their strengths and talents.

James Evans also founded the "Harvest of Hope Awards Banquet," begun in 2006, a black-tie gala that honors "Unsung Heroes" who have made a difference in the lives of youth and families in the Tampa Bay area. Also honored at the banquet are youth and parents who have graduated high school and have successfully completed TBAH's year-round "Leadership Through Education" program. These students have learned to take responsibility for their lives, family, and community and have been accepted at colleges, universities, trade programs or the military.

[In James Evans' words...]
Ordinary people become extraordinary when they persevere through adversity, obstacles and opposition in order to fulfill their life purpose. This is truly the Hero's Journey. Most of us will never experience the roar of an applauding crowd except in our dreams. Nevertheless, all of us can be unselfish heroes in our community. We can do the best we can with what we have and that's all anyone can ask. We can give hope to others by helping the causes for which we are passionate. I hope that my life-changing story will encourage both the young and old to realize it's never too early or too late to apply wisdom or to take action and make a difference!

By 2010, the Tampa Bay Academy of Hope, Inc.(TBAH) had already touched the lives of over 100,000 youth around the country. It is still thriving and striving to help children find their true potential. With the help of the staff of the TBAH, our community partners, and a host of youth development specialists, the Academy has blossomed into a viable organization within the community offering hope to the youngsters of Tampa Bay. Its legacy is the youth who are prepared to face the challenges of the twenty-first century with a positive outlook on life."

---

[80] Iris B. Holton, *"Skills of Hope Youth Leadership Conference 2004."* The Florida Sentinel-Bulletin, 15 Aug 2004.

Since its inception, the Academy has continued to grow and has encouraged and motivated more than 100,000 troubled and under-privileged youth and parents. Almost two dozen private and governmental entities supported the TBAH. In addition, the Academy had several major and local sponsors supporting its efforts: Beef O'Brady's, Coca-Cola, Home Shopping Network, JP Morgan Chase Bank, McDonalds (Casper's Company), Nations Bank, Outback Steakhouse, Publix Charities, Tampa Electric Company, Verizon, and Wachovia-Wells-Fargo Bank. The Academy also received private donations that supplemented its income. Sustainability is achieved through the continued support of the community and corporate collaborators.

There have been many newspaper articles published about myself and the Academy over the years all of which have been favorable and brought attention to the hard work and accomplishments at the TBAH. Below are abbreviated samples to illustrate how the community recognized and applauded our efforts and successes. They have validated the legacy I have left for future generations.

"Study Cites Organization For Work With Juveniles"[81]

"Oftentimes we go about our day following our chosen path... in our mission to succeed...during the periods of struggling we may wonder if our work is reaching the targeted audience.

Recently, that nagging question was answered for James Evans and his staff at the Tampa Bay Academy of Hope, Inc. And the answer came in a method never expected.

The work of the organization was highlighted in the "Florida Youth Suicide Prevention Study," dated September 1999. The report was presented to the Florida State Legislature.

In part the study stated, "Life-affirming and hope-giving environments are the foundation for any youth suicide prevention initiative. Creating school environments where all children and youth feel safe has gained national attention. As our school student population continues to increase in diversity, our school personnel must increase their own diversity competence.

---

[81] Iris B. Holton, "Study Cites Organization For Work With Juveniles," *The Florida Sentinel-Bulletin*, 26 Aug 2003.

"The national Association of School Psychologists believes, "that racism, prejudice, and discrimination are harmful to children and youth because they can have profoundly negative impact on school achievement, self, esteem, personal growth, and ultimately the welfare of all American society." (p.1, Daughtery & Stanhope, 1998).

"We must learn from events such as the three–day youth conference being sponsored by the Tampa Bay Academy of Hope in Tampa…designed to help disadvantaged youth develop life skills and hope," the study asserted.

Evans, who is founder and CEO of the Tampa Bay Academy of Hope, Inc. only recently learned his organization was cited in the study. "For the past five years, we have been trying to save these children, one child at a time. Each year, we attempt to ignite in youth a passion for a better life.

"That is why it is imperative that youngsters, especially those who are labeled 'at-risk', should attend our conference…we have workshop facilitators and mentors who provide living models of the achievements that are possible by living according to positive principles," he said.

Evans continued…"I believe that a young person who has been taught how to develop person[sic] goals and cope with difficult emotions and situations is less likely to consider suicide as solution to his or her problems," Evans said.

In 2008, 100 percent of the seniors enrolled in this program graduated from high school, and in 2009, were currently pursuing post-secondary education. In 2009, TBAH was voted by the Tampa Bay Business Journal as a winner in the category of education for our Leadership Through Education Model. Community, corporate and foundation partners work with TBAH to provide support including volunteerism, financial contributions, and mentoring and health services. TBAH's partners included the City of Tampa, Boy Scouts of America, State Farm Insurance, and Publix Supermarkets.

Later, I was again honored and humbled by the announcement that the TBAH program was selected as a model for a *nationwide* evaluation and implementation. Read on!

"At-Risk Program Draws Attention of FAMU Research Program"[82]

"In 1996, a former professional football player focused his attention on at-risk children, hoping to make a difference in their lives. He created a program that is dedicated to not only helping the youngsters, but their parents as well.

Recently, James Evans, founder of the Tampa Bay Academy of Hope, Inc., was contacted by Dr. Phyllis Gray Ray, Executive Director of the Juvenile Justice Research Institute.

..."We are extremely impressed with your model and would like to evaluate its effectiveness for not only Florida, but also nation-wide implementation."

During a telephone interview, Dr Gray Ray said, "His presentation intrigued us. We'd like to conduct our research using his program as a model. Our institute is new and our primary focus is on the overrepresentation of minorities in the Juvenile Justice System with an emphasis on Black males in specific."

She further stated that Evans's program serves as an excellent model and they hope to begin working with him as early as this summer. We're looking to decrease the number of minorities in the Juvenile Justice System and to keep them from going back. We're very excited about the opportunity to work with him, "Dr. Gray Ray said..."

I'd come a long way from being a poor, simple country boy from Alabama to becoming the founder of an organization that was a potential model for the entire nation!

George Bernard Shaw stated, *"Life is no brief candle to me. It is a sort of splendid torch which I have got a hold of for the moment and I want to make it burn as brightly as possible before handing it on to future generations."*[83] Having a desire to help others is what motivated me to write this book. It is said that our lives are defined not so much by what we get out of life but what we give back. It is defined by what we leave behind for future generations. At the end of my journey in life, I will know that I had contributed to others and that my life had meaning.

For current information about the Tampa Bay Academy of Hope, please visit http://www.tampahope.com

[82] Iris B. Holton, "At-Risk Program Draws Attention of FAMU Research Program," *The Florida Sentinel-Bulletin* 23 Apr 2010.
[83] George Bernard Shaw (1856–1950), Irish writer, playwright, critic, political activist, socialist. Won the Nobel Prize in Literature in 1925 and an Academy Award for writing the 1938 adapted screenplay Pygmalion.

THE IMPORTANCE OF
MENTORS

"Act so as to elicit the best in others and thereby in thy self."
~ Felix Adler (1851-1933), Founder, Ethical Culture movement

William Glasser, the psychologist, was right when he stated: *"We learn 10% of what we read, 20% of what we hear, 30% of what we see, 50% of what we see and hear, 70% of what we discuss, 80% of what we experience, 95% of what we teach others."*

Is it best to plant a young tree in an open field or in a clearing of an old forest? Ecologists tell us that a tree grows better when it's planted in an area with older trees. The reason, it seems, is that the roots of the young tree are able to follow the pathways created by former trees and implant themselves more deeply. Over time, the roots of many trees may actually graft themselves to one another, creating an intricate, interdependent foundation hidden under the ground. In this way, stronger trees share resources with weaker ones so that the whole forest becomes healthier.[84]

People, like trees, can thrive when they are surrounded and supported by more experienced and positive role models or life coaches.[85] At-risk young people are crying out for guidance. There is a dire need in our society for mentors and positive role models—

---

[84] Susan V. Bosak, The Legacy project, *What is a Legacy?*
http://www.legacyproject.org/about/chair.html. Accessed Jan 2011.
[85] The International Coach Federation, describes coaching as an ongoing relationship, which focuses on clients taking action toward the realization of their visions, goals, or desires. Coaching uses a process of inquiry and personal discovery to build the client's awareness and responsibility and provides the client with structure, support, and feedback. The coaching process helps clients both define and achieve professional and personal goals faster and with more ease than would be otherwise possible.

men and women with passion, commitment and dedication—who will recondition and teach our youth a new way of thinking to deal with their pain and neglect. But few step up to the plate. Today's busy lifestyles are challenging. Single moms are busy balancing work with home activities. Family time is diminishing, but society can no longer ignore the voices that cry "Help us!"

The absence of positive role models, mentors or life coaches to effectively influence and restore the worth of at-risk youth leaves a void for which we are paying too high a price. Teachers are dealing more with behavioral issues than with teaching. In many families, both parents are working and their children are often "latch-key kids." No one is home to care for or supervise them after school. There is a popular notion that most teen sex occurs shortly after school lets out, that is, between the hours of 3-6 pm, although one study indicates that a higher percentage occurs between midnight and noon.[86] My observation has been that most inner-city males do not want anything to do with the rearing of their children. They too often have a warped sense of the institution of family and its significance in child rearing. Where have we gone wrong when fathers shun their parental responsibilities? When fathers are absent, extended family members or others are not always there to fill the void or play a significant role in the healthy development of youth. Role models or mentors can step in to demonstrate compassion and understanding, respect and trust, and give them opportunities to be listened to.

The Invisible Man

I grew up with what I refer to as a "father deficiency." I never knew who my biological father was. For some unknown reason, even to this day, my mother has never given me a straight answer when I asked, "Who's my father?" The question probably opened doors to memories she would rather not face. What she did not understand was how this affected me deeply and emotionally. Therefore, it was at an early age that I found myself in search of a father role-model. My older brothers filled some of the gap as best they could, but they were in search of the same thing.

My stepfather, James Monroe, came into my life when I was in the first grade at school until he passed away in 2002 from cancer. He grew up on a farm and was overall a good man who worked to help my mother put food on the table.

---

[86] Of the girls aged 14-16 who participated in this study (all of whom attended school), sex most often occurred between midnight and noon (42 percent of all "events" recorded), followed by 31 percent between 6 p.m. and midnight, 14 percent between 3 p.m. and 6 p.m., and 13 percent between noon and 3 p.m. Sex was most likely to occur on Fridays, Saturdays, and Sundays between midnight and noon. Cited in http://www.thenationalcampaign.org/about-us/PDF/Summer2001update.pdf. Accessed Sept 12, 2011.

However, he was also an alcoholic, was basically illiterate, had served time in prison, and did not know how to bond with me. I felt that he never took the time to listen to or understand me. I imagine that he was never shown how to demonstrate love, so he probably did not know how. He may have been afraid to overstep his bounds and fulfill a father's true role—to be an example to follow. A true father would have dispensed love as well as discipline. In short, I think he was ill-equipped to fill the role of a father in our large family.

On many occasions, the children in the neighborhood would often tease me about who my real father was. Their jokes embarrassed and hurt me because I didn't know who my real father was. They did not realize how their words pierced my young self-worth and made me feel ashamed.

My vision of a father was a man who stood taller than life and would come and rescue me in times of trouble. I imagined that my father would have been there to fight for me at school, protect me from drugs and thugs, and sometimes even from myself. The only thing that did matter was that he wasn't around, and I didn't know where to find him.

To this day, I still don't know who my biological father is, but I would still like to meet the man who gave me life. There are many questions I would have for him if given the opportunity. The first question I would ask him would be why he did not assume his responsibility as a father. However, God always has a way of making things right. I may never have that chance to meet with the man who fathered me, but I have accepted that fact. God interceded on my behalf and became my ultimate Father, one that was not absent, was not afraid and did not shy away from His responsibilities. Many children are raised not knowing their true fathers, and this is where role models and mentors can play a key role in a child's development as it did in mine.

Despite an underprivileged life and troubled youth, I was fortunate enough to have male and female role models and mentors who saw the potential in me and helped me become who I am today. Thanks to the encouragement of one of my older brothers, William, my mother agreed to let me play football and become part of a team. It was then that I began to connect with positive leaders and mentors; this was the most important thing that could have happened to raise my Self-Esteem. My mentors saw in me what I didn't see in myself. They exposed me to ideas and places that broadened my perspective. People telling you that you can succeed does matter. They gave me experiences that changed my life. And the way they lived their own lives mattered; they were my role models, my inspiration, they were my dream-makers and my unsung heroes even at a time when I didn't understand how important they were in shaping my future.

Coaches George Walker and Joe Collins from my Prichard Middle School days pierced my hardened armor and saw the real person that hid inside my shell. We bonded as they encouraged me to participate in the various sporting activities at our school. I came to trust and respect them as they came to listen, understand and believe in my potential.

At Southern University, coaches Otis Washington and Bob Bennett provided me with tough love and pushed me to perform at an elite level. Despite our differences, I knew that deep down they genuinely cared; they gave me a second chance when I quit the team over a dispute about my scholarship. They taught me about humility, how to forgive, make good choices in life, and to never give up.

"No man is your enemy, no man is your friend, but every man is your teacher"
~ Author Unknown

When I entered the NFL, I met "Mr. Motivator," the head football coach of the Kansas City Chiefs. Frank Ganzs was a positive, family-oriented man who would encourage us and always took time out to listen to the players about their issues and concerns. I admired him on and off the field. He inspired me to believe that I could do anything.

In college, I made a commitment to myself that when I got married and had children I would be a father who took his parental responsibility to heart. Today, I not only do this for my own children, but God gave me a vision to help fill the gap for those I meet along the way. I am compelled to reach out and help young people whose lives mirrored my own childhood existence. It was not my goal to become a father figure for young people; however, God guided me into becoming a role model for at-risk young men and women.

I would never have imagined that I would hold self-help and motivational workshops for over 100,000 youth and parents in many states across the country. Through training and development in the Power of Human Worth, I try to inspire youth to avoid violence, gangs, drugs, riots, racism, and any brushes with the law. I strongly encourage them to become better individuals, to go to college and maximize their Worth.

When I started the Academy (TBAH) in 1996, my main focus was to establish a very positive mentoring program that would enrich the lives of students and show them new ways to achieve success in school, college and, subsequently, in the work place. The Academy offered a secure, structured and accessible mentoring program which was key to helping reduce school dropout rates, delinquency and violence among our youth.

We are never isolated from human society, and the effects of our actions always have an impact, great or small, positive or negative, on the lives of others and theirs on us in return. When caring adults share their friendship, knowledge, skills and other resources with less privileged youth, strong relationships may be formed that can be deep and lasting. When mentors or coaches raise the intentional awareness of youth about how to live a satisfactory and content life, how to develop new capabilities and skills, and enhance their emotional competence, youth will ultimately develop resilience, self-efficacy, intimacy and connection in their personal and relational lives. As a result, a sense of well-being, contentment and an overall sense of happiness will emerge.[87] By showing compassion and caring for others, we lift them to a higher level of moral awareness and, in doing so, we also lift ourselves...and the whole community benefits.

People imitate those they admire. The role models that we want for our youth are those who can love them unconditionally and will see the importance and value of every human life. However, there are role models in the community who have lost sight of this. Today, too many leaders are tainted by personal gain, "What's in it for me?" "How do I benefit?" They are insulted when people don't know who they are or what they have accomplished. Do their actions serve others or make matters worse? Do they help others grow as human beings, to become wiser, more independent, and to fulfill their potential? I'm convinced that people can read between the lines with regards as to how much they really care about others. I believe that these poor examples of role models are setting our young people up for failure because they have lost sight of their Human Worth and do not relate to the needs of others.

Not every mentor can be a Mother Teresa, but they must understand and become familiar with all the issues and problems of the community they are helping. It is difficult to address their issues if you have never been in their shoes. This is the difference between being sympathetic versus empathetic. An empathetic mentor has been there or knows innately how to be sensitive to their needs. With good perceptive skills, s/he can see all the good and potential qualities that lie behind the poor behavior of a troubled youth. They have a true understanding of the risks, pain, fears, and setbacks that at-risk youth face on a daily basis. With

---

[87] Talia Ziv, Life Satisfaction & Quality of Life Coaching, http://www.drtaliaziv.com/6.html. Accessed Mar 2011.

true love, understanding and compassion, they focus on the positive inner qualities that already exist.

Story of Anne, 17 years old, high school graduate 2009

> *"If the Tampa Bay Academy of Hope didn't exist, then a lot of students would be without mentors to turn to. Nobody can do it all alone and it is a blessing to know that there are those that care a lot about us to reach out and help us...The mentors that spend their days and nights planning ways to help better our lives sacrifice plenty of things for us.*
>
> *Personally, if the Academy had not been there for me I would have shattered dreams and be going down a long road that I had not yet prepared for. Thanks to the Academy I have learned to channel my negatives into positives and focus on the now and on finding ways to improve my self [sic] and the community I reside in."*

Anne went on to attend a community college in Tampa, Florida.

Many of the children living in the poverty-ridden neighborhoods in Tampa, Florida, are at risk. For the 2009/2010 school year Hillsborough County Public Schools reported that more than 50% of its dropouts were African-American and Hispanic (175 black, 141 Hispanic, of 459 total dropouts). These students struggle with the internal risk factors, such as cognitive deficits, poor problem-solving skills and poor social skills.[88] The Hillsborough County Public Schools system alone cannot address these issues. When a youth participates in positive community activities and develops connections to caring professional adults, the risk of delinquency in even the most troubled communities can be reduced.[89]

There is an inspirational, though fictional, story widely circulated on the internet through emails which shows how much of a difference a mentor can make. It is about little Teddy Stoddard, a messy, unpleasant and disadvantaged child who blossomed under the influence of his teacher, Mrs. Thompson, and went on to become a successful doctor. I'm including it here for those who have never seen or heard of this memorable and moving story and because it demonstrates how all-important or even critical a caring adult can be to a child's future, success and sense of worth.

---

[88] Kenneth G. Roy, "The Systemic Conditions Leading To Violent Human Behavior," *Journal of Applied Behavioral Science*, 36, Dec 2000: 389-407, http://www.jab.sagepub.com/content/36/4/389.full.pdf. Accessed Jan 2011. http://jab.sagepub.com/content/36/4/389.abstract. Accessed Sep 5, 2011.
[89] Office of the Surgeon General, "Youth Violence: A Report of the Surgeon General," (2000), http://www.surgeongeneral.gov/library/youthviolence. Accessed Jan 28, 2010.

There are several versions of this story, some entitled "Three Letters from Teddy", some listing different last names for Teddy. The story was written by Elizabeth Silance Ballard and published in Home Life magazine in 1976. It was not represented as being a true story but rather as a piece of fiction.[90] It was later republished in the magazine with the notation that it was one of the most requested stories in the magazine's history.

The story concerns Teddy Stallard (or Stoddard), who was the kind of kid who strained the mercy of any teacher. His messiness and unpleasantness alienated him from Miss Thompson, his fifth grade teacher, who just didn't like the little brat. In time, she even enjoyed giving Teddy bad grades on his consistently poor homework.

Three Letters From Teddy

"Ashamed as I am to admit it, I took perverse pleasure in using my red pen; and each time I came to Teddy's papers, the cross marks (and they were many) were always a little larger and a little redder than necessary. "Poor work!" I would write with a flourish.

While I did not actually ridicule the boy, my attitude was obviously quite apparent to the class, for he quickly became the class "goat," the outcast—the unlovable and the unloved. He knew I didn't like him, but he didn't know why. Nor did I know—then or now—why I felt such an intense dislike for him. All I know is that he was a little boy no one cared about, and I made no effort in his behalf."

But then Miss Thompson checked Teddy's permanent records:
* *First grade: Teddy shows promise by work and attitude, but has poor home situation.*
* *Second grade: Teddy could do better. Mother terminally ill. He receives little help at home.*
* *Third grade: Teddy is a pleasant boy. Helpful, but too serious. Slow learner. Mother passed away at end of year.*
* *Fourth grade: Very slow, but well-behaved. Father shows no interest.*

With the discovery that he had been a fine student until his mother died of a terminal illness a couple of years earlier, Miss Thompson felt a deep shame over her misjudgment of Teddy. Her guilt worsened when, at Christmastime, the hurting boy gave her some perfume that had belonged to his mother. When Miss Thompson put it on, Teddy told her softly that she smelled just like his mother used to. At that moment the teacher's heart was forever changed toward Teddy.

---

[90] For confirmation that this story is fiction visit http://www.truthorfiction.com/rumors/t/teddy.htm. Accessed Mar 2011.

"I locked the door, sat down at my desk, and wept, resolving to make up to Teddy what I had deliberately deprived him of—a teacher who cared.

I stayed every afternoon with Teddy from the end of the Christmas holidays until the last day of school. Slowly but surely he caught up with the rest of the class. Gradually, there was a definite upward curve in his grades. He did not have to repeat the fifth grade. In fact, his final averages were among the highest in the class, and although I knew he would be moving out of the state when school was out, I was not worried for him. Teddy had reached a level that would stand him in good stead the following year, no matter where he went. He enjoyed a measure of success and, as we were taught in our teacher training courses, 'Success builds success.' "

Her caring devotion paid off as Teddy began to turn his life around.

Years later Miss Thompson received rich rewards for her effort, rewards that came in the form of letters from Teddy. In all his notes, Teddy credited Miss Thompson with changing his life by believing in him.

One letter arrived when Teddy graduated from high school:

Dear Miss Thompson,
I just wanted you to be the first to know. I will be graduating second in my class next month.

Very truly yours,
Teddy Stallard

Four years later, Teddy's second letter came when he graduated with honors from college:

Dear Miss Thompson,
I wanted you to be the first to know. I was just informed that I'll be graduating first in my class. The university has not been easy, but I liked it.

Very truly yours,
Teddy Stallard

"I sent him a good pair of sterling silver monogrammed cuff links and a card, so proud of him I could burst!"

The last letter arrived when he finished medical school and was about to get married:

Dear Miss Thompson,
I wanted you to be the first to know. As of today, I am Theodore J. Stallard, M.D. How about that? I'm going to be married in July, the 27th, to be exact. I wanted to

ask if you could come and sit where Mom would sit if she were here. I'll have no family there as Dad died last year.

Very truly yours,
Theodore F. Stallard, M.D.

"I'm not sure what kind of gift one sends to a doctor on completion of medical school and state boards. Maybe I'll just wait and take a wedding gift, but my note can't wait:

Dear Ted,
Congratulations! You made it, and you did it yourself! In spite of those like me and not because of us, this day has come to you. God bless you. I'll be at that wedding with bells on!

Elizabeth Silance Ballard"[91]

The fact that this story is so widely circulated[92] even to this day shows how many people are touched by it. Preachers even use it in their sermons at church. Many are so moved that they resolve to love the unlovely people in their lives, no matter how much they "bug" them. Some, like the fictional Miss Thompson, are moved enough to make a positive difference in a child's life.

Like Teddy, too many young people grow up with little guidance from parents, relatives and friends and struggle to experience Self-Worth, high Self-Esteem, love, respect, and personal dignity. When they feel worthless, they are vulnerable to crime, drugs, dropping out of school, fear, and more. Many quit school, become pregnant or participate in substance abuse.

They desperately need someone to spend quality time with— to convince them that they have worth and are an asset to mankind. They need someone to teach them about their Human Worth—that with its power anything is possible. Their only limit is what they place on themselves. They can overcome adversity, transform their lives and reach for whatever will help them to lead happy and fulfilling lives.

---

[91] Elizabeth Silance Ballard, "Three Letters from Teddy," *Home Life*, March 1976. Citation: "Teddy Stoddard." http://www.truthorfiction.com/rumors/t/teddy.htm. Accessed Oct 2010.
[92] Mark D. Roberts, "Dan Rather, Meet Teddy Stallard," Oct 11, 2004.
http://www.christianitytoday.com/le/currenttrendscolumns/leadershipweekly/cln41011.html. Accessed Oct 2010.

Why Be a Mentor

My gift lies in serving others. This is what gives my life meaning and purpose. I receive personal fulfillment when I help others; it's a feeling of worthiness—it is the power of Human Worth.

Mentoring creates a feeling of compassion and enables us to care for and serve others. It makes us stronger as a person and allows us to connect to our real self—our Human Worth. In my work with mentoring, I often see how a bond or trust develops between a mentor and a youth; it can create a strong, life-long relationship that allows a youth to change his or her perspective, realize his or her worth and envision a better and brighter future. Many students who participated in the program at the TBAH continue to come back to visit and thank me for being their mentor and being "there" when they needed me the most.

We all need someone to recognize our worth, someone we can look up to as an example and role model. Mentorship activities provide various health and wellness benefits that influence the lives of mentors, students and the community. In August, 2011, I attended the wedding of one of my former TBAH students in Georgia. When I first met him, he was mentally and emotionally unstable, but today, he is a stable and productive member of society and owns his own home. I attribute his success to the intensive mentoring he received from me at the TBAH and afterwards in my own home. Mentoring provides better life satisfaction and physical health for both parties in the relationship who give each other a sense of purpose and satisfaction.

Children are constantly learning from what they see every moment of everyday. We need to provide children, especially those at-risk, with an opportunity to learn and grow in a positive, enriching and nurturing environment. With the proper resources, they can begin to view learning as part of life outside of the four walls of their classrooms. Our children should be introduced to positive role models who demonstrate the importance of education, personal responsibility, leadership, and concern for others. Role models and mentors are essential to foster a partnership between the family, the school and the community to promote the success of its children.

Children of African-American and Latino heritage struggle to keep up with their white peers. In Hillsborough County, Florida, this phenomenon is evident in academic performance, test scores and dropout rates. Even summer vacation time presents a particular challenge for this at-risk group. While many of their middle class peers may be enrolled in summer programs that challenge them both academically and physically, low-income children often find themselves in unsupervised, unstructured environments. At the start of the new school year, they are even further behind. This achievement gap was first reported in the 1960's and is still prevalent today for our socio-economically challenged minority youth.[93]

Children learn what they see. When parents command, "Do as I say, not as I do," they exhibit the kind of mentality which is in direct contradiction of what a mentor or role model truly is. Dr. Dorothy Law Notle sums it up eloquently in her work entitled "Children Learn What They Live" (1972):

"If children live with criticism they learn to condemn.
If children live with hostility they learn to fight.
If children live with fear they learn to be apprehensive.
If children live with pity they learn to feel sorry for themselves.
If children live with ridicule they learn to feel shy.
If children live with jealousy they learn to feel envy.
If children live with shame they learn to feel guilty.
If children live with encouragement they learn confidence.
If children live with tolerance they learn patience
If children live with praise they learn appreciation.
If children live with acceptance they learn to love.
If children live with approval they learn to like themselves.
If children live with recognition they learn it is good to have a goal.
If children live with sharing they learn generosity.
If children live with honesty they learn truthfulness.
If children live with fairness they learn justice.
If children live with kindness and consideration they learn respect.
If children live with security they learn to have faith in themselves and those about them.
If children live with friendliness they learn the world is a place in which to live."

Is the time right for you to step up and become a mentor? Do you have the confidence to assume a mentoring role? Not all of us can be effective mentors, but we all have the potential to be one. Skills for effective mentoring can be developed and optimized through training. But you don't become a mentor in one day—you become one day by day. You "gotta" believe you can and you "gotta" be passionate about what you're trying to achieve in the life of a young person and do it with compassion and love.

[93] First identified in the Report on the Quality of Educational Opportunity in 1966. R. W. Tyler, "The Development Of Instruments For Assessing Educational Progress," In *Proceedings of the 1965 invitational conference on testing problems,* (Princeton, NJ: Educational Testing Service, 1966), 95-105.

"What A Mentor Means To Me" By Isaiah, 17 years old, high school graduate 2010

"Making it to the point [where] i [sic] am now was tough, but i couldn't have done it without the help of James Evans and the Tampa Bay Academy of Hope.

...mentors are people who are there for you no matter what the conditions are and in my condition I needed them badly. i was...struggling tremendously...roaming the streets and everything I knew just started to decelerate inside the heat of my anger. i lost my dad to the prison system because of his anger.

But my mentors told me that my anger can take me to places i don't want to be and potentially ruin my life. Then i realized that i was following in the steps of people that had previously fallen in my life [including his father and older brother].

[My mentors] taught me to use all that anger as positive energy [for] my school work and things i love to do, but the environment i was in and the friends i had ...simply [brought] me down even more. i was doing things that i knew were wrong and things i was taught not to do.

But my mentors never let me out of their grasp. My mentors thought that it was best for me to switch schools because the place I was in [was in] chaos. I couldn't get my grades up and I found myself doing the opposite of what I was in school for. When I transferred my mentors encouraged me...I had to get my grades up and walk across that [graduation] stage and now I'm in the process of completing that assignment.

With 3 months of school left I feel like I've done the impossible...my brother and sister never got their diploma and now I have picked up the torch...I represent all the kids who think they don't have a future. I'm sending a message to them saying that anything is possible....James Evans and the mentors I had were the people who sent that message to me. They took me to different universities showing me what was available to me only if I worked hard. The Tampa Bay Academy of Hope made a big difference in my life and I would have never gotten where I am today without them...and that's what a mentor means to me."

Isaiah was accepted to Hillsborough Community College in Tampa, Florida, during his senior high school year.

Diamonds in the Rough

The word "diamond" is derived from the Greek "Adamas." It means unconquerable. Diamonds are found in a variety of colors: white, black, yellow, brown and others. They represent fortitude, innocence and faithfulness. To the untrained eye, a "diamond in the rough" appears to be worthless, just another ordinary stone. Yet, it is the hardest transparent natural substance known to man. Steel cannot cut a diamond. The only substance that can cut a diamond is another diamond. A diamond possesses unique powers of light reflection. When properly cut, it gathers light within itself, reflecting it back in a shower of fiery brilliance for which they are prized. Only an eye trained to see the beauty within the unpolished stone can appreciate its enormous hidden value.

Our youth are like diamonds in the rough. We must cut and polish them. We must look beyond the exterior to see the exquisite value and intricate beauty locked deep inside of each young person. It is essential that we take the time to honor, explore, unlock, and appreciate the priceless beauty within our youth. They are precious raw gems—sapphires, emeralds, rubies, diamonds—hidden in our communities and waiting to be polished, so that they may boldly embark upon the journey of finding their true Human Worth.

A mentor must possess the ability to recognize the potential in each individual. An effective mentor has patience, love, honesty, trustworthiness, understanding, attentiveness, dependability, kindness, and is a good listener. Above all, s/he must learn to encourage, praise and compliment—even the thoughtfulness of a simple kind word can bring out the inner fiery brilliance of their "gems."

Like an architect, a mentor can visualize a beautiful structure on an empty, vacant lot. The at-risk youth is the vacant lot with nothing on it but their fragile worth. When others don't see or believe in the worth of a troubled youth, a true mentor can see beyond the problematic behavior and see the potential and value inside them. The mentor serves as the architect and hopes to build the foundation of the structure which exemplifies the youth's future. They can visualize how the lives of at-risk or troubled youths can be different and be "turned around" for the better.[94] Ultimately, they will do the right thing, at the right time, for the right reasons, and using the right techniques.

---

[94] A "Turn Around" program exists here in the Hillsborough County School District where one of my Tampa Bay Academy Of Hope students earned the "Turn Around Kid of the Year" 2010 award for his school.

I define a mentor as a coach, teacher, wise advisor, or trusted counselor. With their knowledge and experience, they enable youths to become productive citizens. Mentors are role models who give of themselves with love and compassion. They possess a high level of Self-Worth which is key to why people emulate them. People are eagerly ready to follow persons that understand and exemplify their own Human Worth and even more so when they do it with humility and genuineness. We trust them.

Mentors are made, not born. Certain mentor traits, such as problem-solving, decision-making and creative-thinking, have to be learned and developed and will help mentors be even more effective in coaching at-risk youth. Mentoring as a whole is a very complicated process with both parties constantly reacting and responding to the personal failures and successes that both will experience. Mentors need to be aware of the risks, pain, fears, setbacks, and inconveniences that come with being a mentor of at-risk children. They must be able to provide direction, guidance and management in their quest to help youth recognize and embrace their Human Worth. Adults are the master jewelers who are needed to cut and polish, encourage and model ethical character for our young "diamonds in the rough."

"There is nothing more dangerous than to build a society, with a large segment of people in that society, who feel that they have no stake in it; who feel that they have nothing to lose. People who have a stake in their society, protect that society, but when they don't have it, they unconsciously want to destroy it."
~ Martin Luther King, Jr. (1929-1968)

On April 8, 2010, I was at a local court hearing for a 14-year-old, inner-city, latch-key kid, Carl (not his real name), who was involved with gangs, drugs, guns, and violence. His distorted growth development, emotional problems and violent behavior were directly related to his mother's ongoing verbal abuse and hostility. It was apparent that her unchecked anger had traumatized her son. Carl was growing up with a mother who didn't understand the consequences of her actions—the effect of her violence towards Carl was overwhelming. Internally, he was tattered, confused and afraid. There was no sense of security or caring in his life. His tattoos were symbolic gestures to the injuries, suffering and death that he witnessed all around him. He had a profound loss of trust in his home, the community and the world...and he had lost all hope.

In this case, the issues needing to be addressed were in the home, with his mother and had to be prevented from recurring in the future. However, for many at-risk youth it is academic issues that need to be addressed. Mentoring can provide the support and guidance to help with their academic endeavors by encouraging them to stay in school and graduate. Mentors assist with finding resolutions and can provide these youngsters with many significant benefits, such as enhancing their Self-Worth, Self-Esteem, motivation to succeed, and improving their interpersonal relationships with teachers and family.

While I was actively involved at the Tampa Bay Academy of Hope, my role as a mentor was simply to give the students an awareness and a sense of their fundamental Human Worth and to build on it by helping them transform their thinking, attitudes and behaviors to overcome their daily challenges. I genuinely and sincerely believe that I made a difference in their lives as the following story illustrates:

Story of Sondra, 17 years old, high school graduate 2010

> "Growing up in the inner city, my mom, a single parent, continues to raise me and my five year old brother. [My] father...has been incarcerated since I turned two. Let me tell you about a dramatic experience that happened in my life. About a year ago, I attempted to commit suicide. I swallowed twelve of my grandma's prescription pills and house hold cleaners I found under the sink in the kitchen. At that point in my life, I was feeling lost, confused, and unwanted.
>
> If it wasn't for the grace of God, family, and friends, and the encouraging words from my mentor, I wouldn't be here today....My mentor has been an extended person welcomed to my family, and who has taken the role of my father in his absence. My mentor has filled a void in my life that I didn't know was missing. I have taken a college road trip with my mentor [who]...show [sic] me what it is to live the college life, because of my mentor, I am now ready for college, [I] scored a 1220 on my SAT's, and plan on pursuing my dreams. "

Sondra went on to attend a community college in Tampa, Florida.

By being the role models that they are, by doing all that they can, by all the means that they can and in all the ways that they can, mentors teach youth how to recognize and connect to their inner worth and understand that they are more than just an ordinary stone, but a diamond hidden in the rough. As Sondra's story above demonstrates, mentors leave a legacy in the lives of the young people with whom they interact. They enable their students to see the importance, value, meaning, and purpose of their lives.

Traits of a Good Mentor

"When you study great teachers... you will learn much more from their caring and hard work than from their style."
~ William Glasser, psychologist

Mentors must possess a sense of empathy which enables them to look at a situation through the eyes of another and gain a far deeper understanding of that person. Mentors who show and give respect to others have the ability to connect with people in a most unique way and are the most successful in helping them to feel understood. By adjusting their style to fit each particular situation, they meet the needs of others and bring out the best in young people.

Mentors must strive to be the most positive influence on those who look up to and admire them. Youth don't want to know how much you know; they want to see how much you care. This realization is critical to being a mentor. At the Tampa Bay Academy of Hope, where I established an intensive mentoring program, I was compelled to be a genuine role model for my students as my past mentors had been for me. I wanted to help shape their characters by teaching them to realize that trust, honor, respect, integrity, and credibility are important to who they are.

At the Academy, we also recruited volunteers who were committed to becoming mentors and had the character worthy of a child's respect in order to impact them effectively. We trained them to be accountable for the ways in which they would influence the lives of our young students. The volunteers were required to observe how I interacted one on one and with a group of students. They also attended meetings where both the student(s) and the parent(s) were present to observe how I interacted with them in a way that fosters their innate worth. The volunteers were taught not to ever disrespect or belittle the youth or diminish whatever little worth the youth may be struggling with. We don't want feelings of worthlessness to emerge or to inflict our fears upon the youth that we've been given the opportunity to influence.

Mother Teresa embodied compassion and empathy and led her life with a caring heart. She did not live for fame or riches, but cared for the hungry, sick, dying, and poor. She knew her worth and recognized and understood the worth of those she so lovingly cared for. She possessed a pure, unmoving, unshakeable spirituality that was balanced with the reality of everyday life. Her self-sacrifice enabled others to meet their own deepest need: to feel a part of a larger shared humanity. She was one of the world's greatest and most effective role models.

If there is ever a perception that an individual is mentoring for their own satisfaction or gain or more out of obligation than compassion, then people will see right through them. If a mentor is more concerned about their own image and success, this will cause resistance and resentment in those they are trying to mentor. Effective mentors have openness to what others experience and do so without reservation or judgment...or by trying to change it. They have a deep appreciation for what it is like to "be in another's shoes." This empathy is a significant factor in perceiving the Human Worth in others and helps to establish a deep connection of mutual vulnerability and intimacy. By displaying love, respect, empathy and compassion, mentors can easily win the trust and approval of their students.

To be most effective, mentors should tailor their style to fit their students and thus stay humble while encouraging them to achieve their goals. It is important for mentors to show the "soft side" of their character. Mentors can be soft-spoken yet still be a great source of strength. Blending the softer skills—trust, empathy and genuine communication—with the tougher skills needed to keep people on task is essential to working with at-risk youth.

Story of Phylisha, 17 years old, high school graduate 2009

"I would be another statistic if it were not for Tampa Bay Academy of Hope. Yes, I was classified as a problem child, adopted at birth and suffering with anger problems because I felt unwanted. No one thought I could or would make it. Nevertheless, I can now tell you I did. I am a seventeen-year-old graduate of Blake High School and in the fall of 2009, I will be attending Florida Memorial University or Edward Waters College.

Although I had always been involved in other organizations whose primary goal was to help me get into college, after becoming a part of Tampa Bay Academy of Hope I realized my true worth. Without Tampa Bay Academy of Hope, I would still feel that I have no particular purpose in life. I would not have been exposed to the opportunities I have such as The Leadership Tour; I have significantly sharpened my leadership skills by participating in Tampa Bay Academy of Hope.

After my father and grandmother died March 20 and March 22, of 2007, I felt abandoned with nowhere to go. But through positive male role models such as Mr. Tallie, Mr. Mark and Mr. James, I found in them the father figure I missed. If there was no Tampa Bay Academy of Hope, students like me would be lost with no hope or any plans for a better life.

I have enjoyed myself while being a part of such a program like this. Particularly, not only have I met many new people, but also I have gained knowledge that will help me now and throughout my future. Students like me are not always given a chance and often are ignored. But because of Tampa Bay Academy of Hope I can truly say, "I AM NOT FORGOTTEN."

Phylisha went on to attend Florida A & M University.

Mentors must maintain a passion and should guide by example. If a coach stands idly by and yells at a youth to work harder, s/he will lose credibility with every word because s/he is not doing the very thing they are asking the youth to do, i.e., to work hard. But if they walk around showing interest, making corrections and spotting them, then their active participation serves as a positive example of what is expected of them. Most importantly, a good mentor must:

1. Be a good listener. Take the time to listen effectively to their concerns. In many cases, the mentor is the only person that the student has identified as one who will listen to their problems. Be open to what your student can teach you or share with you.

2. Be encouraging. Do not motivate by force or guilt. Bring out their best by empowering them to do for themselves. Be enthusiastic—it's contagious. Help identify your student's talents, strengths and assets. Help your student use mistakes as learning experiences.

3. Be assertive and fair. Say what needs to be said without being unkind. Tell the truth as you see it, openly and frankly. Be fair—they'll notice if you're not.

4. Be decisive. Know what needs to be done and make timely, even difficult, decisions when necessary. Be firm. Have your student assume responsibilities and hold him or her accountable.

The process of becoming a mentor also involves many more details and guidelines which, while essential, are also fairly simple to understand and employ:

1. Set short and long-term goals. Remind the student that if s/he fails to plan, s/he is really planning to fail. Mentors need to outline and fine-tune a game plan to fit the youth's

needs and be able to keep up with changing technology to be effective in relating to what youth are interested in. Then, as each stage of the plan becomes a reality for the youth, the mentor must follow through to ensure that it remains intact.

2. Help the student identify the positive things in his/her life.
3. Employ role-playing as a technique for solving problems.
4. Help the student to develop personal interests outside of school. This might entail field trips to the library, a work site or other approved places.
5. Help the student become more involved in all aspects of school.
6. Be sincere, committed and punctual for scheduled meetings.
7. Develop a level of trust with the student. A trusting relationship is the foundation for a successful and often lasting relationship.

A good mentor guides, not forces, his students. If I say, "You're not gonna like it, but it's time for you to learn one of the hardest skills in football—to block and tackle," I would immediately cause them to be discouraged and turn them off. If, however, I excitedly explain to them that they are now advanced enough to begin learning one of the most important and challenging skills in football, I will pass that same excitement along to them…and get a different result. A mentor should show how everything, even problems, can be viewed as exciting challenges to overcome, not as obstacles that are insurmountable.

Factors for Successful Mentoring

Discipline and Commitment

In my role as a mentor, I understand the importance of commitment and a willingness to take on the full responsibility that mentoring requires. Relatively few, however, realize the importance of self-discipline to ensure that they stay on track and follow through at every step of the way with their students. Role models and mentors of children carry a heavy responsibility because children are very impressionable and never forget what is said, told or promised to them. My own children say to me all the time, "But

Daddy, you said…" Having the discipline to act consistently in the life of a young person will create the most successful results.

Thomas Edison once said, "There is no substitute for hard work." But the work of a mentor is not hard when they are disciplined and apply it wisely when needed. A mentor should not be afraid to delegate responsibilities to youth or to provide them with discipline. They should be goal-oriented and set deadlines, helping youth to strive to meet them. The purpose of setting a deadline is a form of self-discipline, and it motivates both the mentor and the youth to stay on track as much as possible. Discipline, hard work, assertiveness, and relentless attention to the issues that concern youth are the tools needed to effectively influence and restore the worth of youth.

Communication

"The problem with communication is the illusion that it's taking place"
~ George Bernard Shaw (1856-1950), Irish writer, playwright

Good communication is important in any relationship. In a mentoring relationship, where the goal is to influence and persuade others, good communication is essential. Communication is a two-way process that involves sending and receiving a message. Listening and speaking are equally important. While listening provides a learning opportunity, young people have only short attention spans usually lasting for about 20-30 minutes. Listening depends on how the message is delivered and also on how the message is received. How they see you and your message will determine whether they will like what you have to say. Use language that's easy to understand. Give concrete explanations. Your language, the word-pictures you use and the channels through which you communicate the message are of critical importance. However, body language, tone of voice and facial expression speak more than words about how they will receive the message. How you deliver the message is just as important as the message itself; it must be understandable, positive and believable.

"If you talk to a man in a language he understands, that goes to his head. If you talk to him in his own language, that goes to his heart."
~ Nelson Mandela

A mentor who wants to be an effective communicator will consider the personalities and attitudes of their students in order to make the message as persuasive as possible. When communicating to others, credibility is one of the most important traits a mentor can possess. Their audience must believe what they have to say. When we send a message to others, it is essential that we say what we mean and mean what we say.

We don't know for certain how effectively we have communicated unless there is some sort of feedback from those who are receiving the message. We get feedback by observing their reactions to what we are saying. Are they looking at you intently or are they playing with their fingernails or staring off into space? Feedback also happens when they verbally respond to the message and are given an opportunity to speak. Your message should be interesting enough to stimulate their interest and provoke questions.

We live in a world where we must interact with hundreds, if not thousands, of people in our lifetimes. Today's youth have few opportunities to develop traditional communication skills. But these skills are essential—without them youth may act out by becoming violent or by isolating and shutting themselves down and avoiding interactions with family and school and they will fail to achieve their potential. Effective communication enables them to confidently share their thoughts at home, school, work, church, and in social situations and, in turn, to connect to their Human Worth.

Conflict Resolution

Conflict is a part of all relationships. Conflict arises because of different values, goals, ideas, or interpretations. When a conflict situation arises, mentors should not get defensive or over-react but should show interest in getting to the root cause, tackle the problem objectively and not blame the student. Not discussing conflict always makes the situation worse. Discuss the matter, if need be, with family and friends. Sometimes, conflict is beneficial to finding the best solution. It is destructive when the focus is on winning (like the mentor saying that they are right and the youth is wrong).

Troubled youth are usually unaware of the habits they apply in conflict situations. Two concerns come into play in any conflict: personal goals and keeping good relationships. Unfortunately, the latter is usually not the priority; they may resort to animal-like violent behavior in dealing with others and are more concerned about their "bad ass" gangster images. How much importance we give to each of these concerns affects how we act in a conflict, such as resolving problems, fighting for the last word, saying everything is okay when it isn't, not wanting to talk about it, serving up "put-downs," and gossiping about people.

When troubled youth don't want to talk about it, a mentor should resist the urge to push, but, instead, use an understanding voice and tone and maybe even set a specific time to discuss the differences. Mentors have to resist any urge to control the situation and instead help them to reason and show them the alternatives to their otherwise self-destructive behavior. Keep in mind that it is more effective to share your knowledge rather than to give advice when working out problems. Ask for opinions and participation in decision-making. When one avenue fails to yield the desired response, it may become necessary to devise a new plan and start from the beginning.

A Memorial Day Incident at Adventure Island

Busch Gardens' Memorial Day event at Adventure Island in Tampa, Florida—a traditional gathering day for many of the middle and high schools in the area—attracted over 8,000 youth and young adults from the ages of 9-24 from the Tampa Bay area in 2000. After the park had surpassed its capacity of about 5,000 guests, it closed the entry points. But the surplus youth illegally invaded the park, tearing down the park's front gates, fences and barricades to do so. These wild and unmanageable gangs caused a riot with stampedes of youth running, but also trampling on children and adults. They watched or participated in many bloody gang fights taking place all over the Park. They harassed and fought with park guests, stole from the concessions, had public sex in the water areas and bathrooms, snatched off girls' bathing suit tops and destroyed all of the park's many flower gardens. They also fought with police officers. The Park had already hired 50 off-duty police officers for the expected event, but had to call in many additional police and paddy wagons to arrest and haul off the disorderly offenders. In a 12-hour span from 7am to 7pm, these unruly gangs had destroyed a multi-million dollar Park.

In the two succeeding years, the Florida Sentinel published a series of articles which not only brought this event to the attention of the public, but served to attract more gangs and even pedophiles who were lured by the presence of so many young people in one place. The Florida Sentinel lambasted Adventure Island management for failing to resolve the conflicts between the unruly youths and authority and having hundreds of youths arrested for a variety of criminal charges: disorderly conduct, trespassing, battery, concealed weapons, assault on an officer, lewd and lascivious behavior, theft...and the list goes on.

In 2002, I was contacted by the City of Tampa and the mayor's African-American Advisor Council asking if I would meet with the Chief of Police, his executive officers, the Florida Sentinel, and Adventure Island management. I agreed to discuss a solution to remedy the Park's crisis and to avoid drawing national attention to the Park's inability to control disruptive crowds of disorderly youth and *shutting down the Park completely (for the Memorial Day event). One reason for the crisis was that many parents just dropped off their children and left, leaving their young children unattended. My recommendation was to have adult supervision in key places throughout the day. I suggested using 300 of my Tampa Bay Academy of Hope adult mentors in two shifts—this large number of "chaperones" would reduce the aggressive behavior and ensure a safer day for all guests at the Park. I taught the mentors how to interact effectively with youth throughout the day, being proactive in facilitating good behavior. I also insisted that they would be the first ones to address and confront any disruptive youths and to diffuse any escalating incident before police would use any force in enforcing civil ordinances. Based on the information I provided, the park instituted a new rule that required children under the age of 12 to be accompanied by a parent, adult or legal guardian.*

The Park is now celebrating Memorial Day with few incidents because of the presence of the many mentors who diffuse confrontations between overly zealous youth and the local authorities. When youth fail to comply with the rules of the Park, instead of being arrested and loaded into paddy wagons, the offenders are escorted out by mentors, Park security guards and police officers.

A follow-up Florida Sentinel article "Memorial Weekend a Success for Theme Park," reported that despite a crowd of 6,800 people, thanks to the presence of the mentors the Park didn't have any major problems and the kids were well-behaved. By working together with members of the community, conflicts were greatly minimized, and the event went smoothly. And mentors had made the difference.

Trust

"The best way to understand people is to listen to them."
~ Dr. Ralph G. Nichols (1907–2005)[95]

Mentoring is open-ended dialogue and listening, rather than forcing your point of view down somebody's throat. Rare is the parent who understands the value of listening—without interruption—to a child sharing their thoughts. A mentor can fill that void by being there to listen without judgment or a self-serving agenda. By listening first, we build trust.

---

[95] Dr. Ralph G. Nichols served for decades as the Chairman of the Department of Rhetoric, Univ. of Minnesota. His 1948 Doctoral Dissertation at the Univ. of Iowa identified the groundbreaking factors that differentiated the behaviors of effective and ineffective listeners which established a benchmark for all future Listening scholars and practitioners.

Trust is a firm reliance on the integrity, ability or character of a person. People with character do the right thing, at the right time. Trust is not given but earned. Young people react to deeds versus words; how you live your life versus what you say. You can gain trust by acting with character and facilitating the goals and visions of your students. With trust, a lasting relationship may be born.

To gain trust, not only should mentors keep their promises and show respect, but whatever they envision for their students must be real. People will trust when they believe that their interest is at the heart of your goals and objectives. Having the knowledge of who the youth is, where they want to go and how they will allow you to help them get "there"—remember, there is a "there"—helps with your involvement with young people. This knowledge is helpful when there is a breakdown of communication and you are not sure what to do.

As young people learn to trust and follow you, remember that you must be willing to accept criticism and allow them to scrutinize your genuineness. You may at times have to defend yourself and your actions while staying committed. It's important to be flexible and evaluate each situation or circumstance. It's important to know or learn how and when to draw the line and when to adapt. You must be persistent without being overbearing and maintain a positive attitude. This attitude is contagious and will encourage them to be themselves.

When mentors demonstrate positive behavioral traits, eventually the at-risk youth will recognize them and begin to learn about trust and credibility. In order to be a good example, whatever rules, regulations or even suggestions are made for the youth, the mentor must also be willing to follow. If they expect youth to work hard, they must do the same. If they expect punctuality for meetings or practices, they must also be on time. If they expect respect, they must show that it is never acceptable to disregard common rules of courtesy and respect for others.

I am a living testimony to the difference having a mentor can make in your life. Finding a good mentor will help you to be the best you can be. I *know!* My experiences with them have transformed me and my life.

The TBAH Mentoring Program

"Education is the most powerful weapon which you can use to change the world."   ~ Nelson Mandela

TBAH was structured on a Leadership Through Education program within which mentoring was a key component.[96] Academy mentors were committed to expending the time and energy necessary to help a young person get his/her life back together academically, socially, mentally, and physically. An Academy mentor was more than just a role model; s/he was there, most of all, as a friend.

My program helped youth transition from lives of hopelessness, poverty and dependence to a future life of optimism, independence and self-sufficiency. The activities, combined with classroom instruction, supportive services and parent involvement, encouraged positive youth development and diminished inappropriate behaviors: 80% of enrolled students attained attendance rates of 85% or better and 80% improved their behavior by reducing the number of suspensions.

The Florida Department of Education estimated that 80% of at-risk students fail to graduate from high school. Hillsborough County Public Schools reported that its dropout rates for the 2006/2007 school year were among the highest in the state of Florida. The Academy's mentor program addressed this tragic issue successfully. Mentors worked with these disadvantaged students in the "belly of the beast," that is to say, that they were in the trenches with them—surrounded by crime, drugs and violence.

By providing additional learning opportunities to those needing it, the mentor program made a world of difference by enabling 98% of our students to graduate. Without a diploma, youth are more likely to face a future of poverty, crime and drugs and are less likely to become productive members of society. Providing numerous, additional opportunities to meet various community leaders at the county, state and national levels exposed them to the many resources available to them. Touring colleges and universities throughout the State of Florida improved their social networking capabilities and inspired them to go to college. Most of these youth went on to attend state universities as first-generation college students.

---

[96] Information relevant to when I was active in the TBAH. *See Appendix B for the four-step approach used to accomplish the mission of TBAH.*

In the summer of 2010, I retired from the TBAH as Executive Director to focus my efforts on the pursuit of other passions— inspiring, motivating and encouraging others by giving presentations and workshops to larger audiences of companies, corporations, church groups, and other institutions. I also charted a new course towards fulfilling another and larger dream—writing this book and re-building my company, Eagle Quest Group, Inc., (http://www.eaglequestgroup.com/), so that I could teach the "Fundamentals of The Power of Human Worth" nationwide.

Community Service

"The greatest essential in life is service to others, so keep serving others."
~ James M. Evans

Martin Luther King, Jr. once stated, *"Everybody can be great because anybody can serve. You don't have to have a college degree to serve. You don't have to make your subject and verb agree to serve. You only need a heart full of grace...a soul generated by love."* Dr. King was describing what a mentor is. An essential component of being a mentor is to serve the needs of others. A mentor has the gift to serve and influence others in a positive way. Service to at-risk youth is the willingness to lend a helping hand without looking for recognition or rewards. It is a genuine act of compassion to help in times of need by bringing a ray of hope and light into the lives of less fortunate young people. Service is an unselfish act that is given freely and without coercion. It is about reaching out to others without waiting to be asked, without being judgmental and without making comparisons to others.

I have never been the type to just sit on the sidelines. I was compelled by my own worth to become involved in my community and help impact and improve the worth of others. With dedication and commitment, I went out into the world, confident in helping others to bear their burdens. Service is the willingness to reach down to help someone up. It's knowing when to speak and when to listen. Service is knowing when to provide and when to show someone how to provide for themselves. Service is demonstrating that someone does care and that no one is alone. We can change the world one person at a time and be a lifesaver in a sea of turmoil.

TBAH students serving the community on Thanksgiving

All of us can serve by being a role model or mentor for the next generation. We need more positive role models, mentors and leaders for their guidance and encouragement to reduce social and economic problems and improve housing and educational opportunities. When community leaders fail to have compassion, hope and love of their fellow citizens, they are failing to see the value of Human Worth in each and every member of their community.

There is much work to be done in our community and around the world. The percentages of teen sex and drug use, the high school dropout rate and teenagers attempting suicide in the United States are at all-time highs. We serve them with too little resources, too little support and only a very small percentage of us are taking on the challenges that others refuse to.

If community leaders do not take their responsibilities to improve the quality of life for others, then incidents like the following will always occur:

- Violence
  - Everyday in America, 135 children bring a gun to school. (Children's Defense Fund 2008)
  - More than 208,000 teens aged 12 to 17 were reported as victims of family violence in 1990. (National Center on Child Abuse and Neglect)

- Teen Suicide
  - Every day in America, 6 teenagers commit suicide. (Children's Defense Fund 2008)

- Smoking
  - Most adolescents who have smoked at least 100 cigarettes in their

lifetime report that they would like to quit, but are not able to do so. Each day, more than 4,800 teens smoke their first cigarette. Almost 2,000 of these will become regular smokers—that's 720,000 annually. One-third of these children smokers will eventually die of smoking-related illnesses.
- At least 4.5 million adolescents are current smokers. 22.4% of all 12th graders smoke cigarettes daily. (American Lung Association, 1999)

- Drinking
  - Every day in America, 437 children are arrested for drinking or drunken driving. (Children's Defense Fund 1995)
  - 4.2 million persons aged 16 to 20 reported driving under the influence of alcohol or illegal drugs during the past year. About 169,000 of these persons (4%) reported that they had been arrested and booked for DUI/DWI involving alcohol or drugs in the past year. (SAMHSA 2003)[97]

- Drugs
  - Every day in America, 211 children are arrested for drug abuse. (Children's Defense Fund 1995)
  - About 1.5 million youth (7.6% of the youth who had not used an illicit drug previously) used at least one illicit drug in the past year. (SAMHSA 2005)[98]

- Broken Homes
  - Every day in America, 2,989 see their parents divorce. (Children's Defense Fund 1995)
  - More than 50% of children are in a single parent household at some point in their lives. (Demuth and Brown, 2004)[99]

- Teen Pregnancy
  - 12.8 % of all births are to teenage mothers. (US Census Bureau, US National Center for Health Statistics, 1997)
  - Every day in America, 1,295 teenagers give birth; 1,106 teenagers have abortions; and 7,742 teens become sexually active. (Children's Defense Fund)
  - Eight in ten teens report that their pregnancy was unplanned.

[97] "The NSDUH Report: Driving Under the Influence (DUI) Among Young Persons," Substance Abuse & Mental Health Services Administration, U.S. Department of Health & Human Services, (2003), http://www.oas.samhsa.gov/DWI.htm. Accessed Aug 24, 2011.
[98] "The NSDUH Report: Depression and the Initiation of Alcohol and Other Drug Use among Youths Aged 12 to 17," Substance Abuse & Mental Health Services Administration, U.S. Department of Health & Human Services, 2005, http://www.oas.samhsa.gov/2k7/newUserDepression/newUserDepression.cfm. Accessed Aug 24, 2011.
[99] S. Demuth and S. Brown, "Family Structure, Family Processes and Adolescence Delinquency: The Significance of Parental Absence versus Parental Gender," Journal of Research in Crime and Delinquency, 41:1 (Feb 2004): 58-81, http://jrc.sagepub.com/content/41/1/58.short. Accessed Aug 30, 2011.

(National Campaign to Prevent Teen and Unplanned Pregnancy 2006)

- STDs
  - Every day in America, 623 teenagers get syphilis or gonorrhea. (Children's Defense Fund)
  - Nearly half of the 19 million new STDs each year are among young people aged 15–24 years (CDC 2009)[100]

- Runaways
  - Every day in America, 3,288 children run away from home (Children's Defense Fund)
  - Between1.6 and 2.8 million youth runaway each year. (National Runway Switchboard 2011)[101]

- Drop-outs
  - Approximately 5 percent of teens drop out prior to high school graduation. Hispanic students have the highest dropout rate in the nation, followed by African American students.
  - In 2008, 18.3 percent of Hispanic teens ages 16 to 24 dropped out of school. For the same age group in 2008, 9.9 percent of black students dropped out and only 4.6 percent of white students. (National Center for Education Statistics (NCES))

There is nothing anyone can say or do to deter me from being a strong advocate for people struggling with behavioral and social problems and who have lost sight of their Human Worth. Not speaking up at the right time is a tragedy if it leaves others vulnerable. I feel compelled to be a voice for those who cannot speak up for themselves. The newspaper article excerpted below demonstrates how one person—anyone—can make a difference in the lives of others. Unfortunately for the youth in this case, it was his death that spurred a change in "the system."

"One Citizen's Quest For Justice"[102]

"After seeing a video tape of a teen's boot camp beating, a Tampa man writes to the state Medical board.

The former NFL player and Tampa activist tells kids at his nonprofit organization that one person can make a difference.

---

[100] Center for Disease Control, *Sexual Risk Behavior: HIV, STD and Teen Pregnancy Prevention*, 2009, http://www.cdc.gov/HealthyYouth/sexualbehaviors/. Accessed Aug 24, 2011.
[101] "NRS Statistics on Runaways," In National Runaway Switchboard, 2011.
http://www.1800runaway.org/learn/research/third_party. Accessed Aug 24, 2011.
[102] Abbie Vansickle, "One citizen's quest for justice," St Petersburg Times [FL], 17 Jun 2007, http://www.sptimes.com/2007/06/17/Hillsborough/One_citizen_s_quest_f.shtml. Accessed Oct 2010.

Now, he has proof. The state Medical Examiners Commission meeting last week to remove the Bay County medical examiner featured all the usual players in the widely publicized boot camp case. Sheriffs, lawyers and legislators weighed in on the reasons to oust Dr. Charles F. Siebert Jr.

But there was a new name in the case, right there on the meeting agenda: complaint by James Evans. Evans didn't attend. He didn't even know about the meeting or that he'd help start the inquiry. He wrote the letter more than a year ago.

Evans, 43, is the executive director of the Tampa Bay Academy of Hope, a nonprofit group aimed at improving the lives of at-risk youths and their families. Evans also organized a town hall meeting two years ago on the fairness of the legal system in the wake of two controversial local court decisions.

Evans said he wrote the letter about Siebert after watching the videotape of boot camp guards roughing up a Panama City teen. As a father of two and a local community organizer, the former Buccaneers player was angered by the guards' actions.

"This mother sent her child to the camp thinking that they were going to make her child better," he said. "It devastated me to watch a child get beaten down and murdered in that way."

When he watched a medical examiner blame Martin Lee Anderson's death on sickle cell trait, not the beating, he wrote to the Medical Examiners Commission. He signed his letter "James M. Evans, Servant of the People."

Evans said no one ever told him, but his letter started the state's Medical Examiners Commission inquiry into Siebert, according to the Florida Department of Law Enforcement. That investigation led to the commission's unanimous vote last week to remove the doctor from his post. Evans had no clue his letter had such an impact.

"Wow. My letter was used? You're kidding," he said when he learned the news. "Nobody contacted me. I'd forgotten all about that letter." He said he figured dozens of people around the state wrote in to demand an investigation. He figured wrong.

His was one of two letters received by the commission. The other letter was written by a state legislator. "That's frightening that nobody else did this," Evans said. "Wow, I thought mine would just be another one in a stack."

At the modest headquarters of the Academy of Hope, in a storefront office near Ybor City, Evans thumbed through the commission's report. Evans' eyes widened as he read that Siebert had put false information in the report, that he wrote about descriptions of organs he never dissected. "He needed to resign," Evans said. "I'm grateful that they listened."

This incident occurred because no one at the time of the beating took a stance to uphold what was morally right—to protect the life of an innocent human being that was placed in the care of the state..."for the people."

We all live, work or play either in a city, town or rural area where we can participate in local events and activities, attend school and associate with other local citizens. Leaders, role models and mentors can reinforce the rights, duties and obligations of citizenship; they can teach youth that they have a right to attend school, get a job, own a business, vote in elections at the proper age, serve in the country's military, and be safe. These leaders can also educate youth about their duties and obligations to follow the law, serve on a jury, pay taxes, keep their community safe, and assist where and when needed.

Caring and helpful community members who sacrifice their time, talent and treasures deserve our respect and recognition. At the end of the TBAH fiscal year, I felt it was important to recognize not only the young people in the Academy's program but also to recognize the "unsung" heroes in our community—people who went above and beyond the call of duty to help those in need. For 13 years, we paid tribute to community leaders and organizations for giving of themselves for the benefit of the Tampa Bay Academy of Hope. A local newspaper covered the following:

"James Evans and Tampa Bay Academy of Hope Holds Faces of Hope Black Tie Gala and Fundraiser 2009"[103]

"On June 27th, the Tampa Bay Academy of Hope held their 13th annual Celebrating Faces of Hope gala and fundraiser at the A La Carte Event Pavilion in Tampa.

The black tie dinner and awards show, which was emceed by Kathy Fountain and Frank Robertson, formerly of FOX 13, honored 17 previously at-risk high school seniors who graduated this year and are now going on to higher education, as well as the "unsung heroes" of 2009 who made a difference in the lives of Tampa's children and families in the past year.

Governor Charlie Crist says of the Academy, "With the help of organizations like Tampa Bay Academy of Hope, we can provide a better future for our children." The Academy of Hope has assisted with leadership training, mentoring, job

---

[103] Heidi Lux, "James Evans and Tampa Bay Academy of Hope Holds Faces of Hope Black Tie Gala and Fundraiser 2009," Tampa Bay Informer-Clearwater, 14 Jul 2009.

placement and scholarship development for over 100,000 youths since its inception, and is also active in the field of human rights."

Changing Our Communities

"People don't hate change—they hate the promise of change unfulfilled."
~ Anonymous

When I was a kid living in the inner city, I lost sight of my value and importance and resorted to crimes and violence. Today, when I see youth struggling the same way as I did, I can relate to their pain and suffering. If you've never experienced hopelessness or despair, you would find it difficult to relate to why it is so significant for me to want to change our communities. I have fought in the "belly of the beast" as a "warrior" in the war to reverse the cycle of poverty, crime and educational underachievement of our children. I have personally assisted troubled youths from the jail cell to the courtroom, from the classroom to the home and in the community at large. I have helped and supported their parents by reaching out tirelessly to hundreds of organizations in order to obtain financial assistance for them.

I'm compelled to help youth turn away from trouble and face who they really are—divine human beings endowed at birth with the power of Human Worth, individuals with the power to change their behaviors and become productive citizens.

The St Petersburg Times (Florida) published an article entitled, "With soft words, turning kids—from trouble,"[104] that I've excerpted below as an example of a problem that exists all over the country. It shows how one person can give a community a new perspective and change how it typically responds to incidents of youth "trouble." More importantly, it reveals how mentors make a difference in the lives of troubled youth.

"The scene reminded James Evans of days he thought had passed. Hip-hop boys and fly girls were spilling out of Club Bling after midnight and going down the street instead of going home creating an unfriendly atmosphere in the Ybor City [Tampa, FL] entertainment district. A few of the bar owners complained to police.

"It reminded me of what took place back in the early '60s," said Evans, who knew a lot of the Club Bling kids from his work as executive director of Tampa Bay

---

[104] Ernest Hooper, "With Soft Words, Turning Kids—From Trouble," St Petersburg Times [FL], 10 Sept 2004.

Academy of Hope. "The humongous horses were standing over and frightening children."

Police said they were just doing their job. The bar owners said their concerns were legitimate. Evans viewed it differently. "There wasn't a major problem with kids," Evans said. "There was no alcohol being served, no violence going on..."

Last month, Evans and other community leaders met with the Mayor and other concerned officials. At the suggestion of Evans, they crafted a plan to have mentors greet the kids at night's end and shepherd them home or until someone picked them up. To deal with the youngest kids, who were tagging along with older brothers and sisters, Evans circulated more than 2,000 fliers throughout various neighborhoods alerting parents to the problem.

Now, most kids are getting home instead of getting arrest records. By adding sensitivity and understanding to the mix, it appears the problem has waned. "We have to invest in children or we're going to have to invest more...in prisons," Evans said.

Helping youths is more than talk to Evans, and people are listening. "If we see them as they are, they'll only become worse," Evans said. "If we look at them as what they could be, then they'll become what they should be."

This event is just one example of how I have fought in my local community to shape the character of the next generation of our youth and earned a reputation as a youth advocate. Lack of concern for the community is unacceptable to me. I even risked my career as a community organizer when I confronted the Chief of Police and admonished him about his use of confiscated drug monies. Since he was in office, the monies were no longer shared among the many organizations helping the community. He gave the monies only to the Police Athletic League, a police-supported organization, and no longer supported the rest of the struggling community organizations. I addressed the issue but to no avail.

However, I maintained my self-resiliency and determination. When I was chair of the African-American Advisory Council for the Mayor of Tampa, I urged her to give more support for minority businesses as a way to help the at-risk community. Instead, she accepted my resignation and it became a local media frenzy. But, again, it was to no avail.

I continually become involved with reducing the violence and poverty that plague my community and diminish the worth of its youth. I do it by encouraging mentors, educating our children, advising their parents and grandparents, assisting the elderly and the sick, and feeding the hungry and the homeless. I simply find it gratifying when young people go on to make a success of their lives. My vision for these members of my community is to see them empowered with confidence, determination and success. I'm advocating with only genuine motives because someone did it for me, and I want to pay it forward. I don't seek recognition or attention. I apply the passion, power and purpose burning deep within me to help our youth find their essence, their own Human Worth, i.e., what gives their lives meaning and purpose.

In March 2010, I served on the panel of Michael Baisden's (a national syndicated radio show host)[105] One Million Mentors Campaign presentation when he visited in Tampa, Florida. I am proud to share with my readers that during the presentation, it was announced that the Tampa Bay Academy of Hope was the sole Tampa recipient to be awarded the sum of $10,000 to support its mentoring program. The award was a big win for TBAH enabling the students to learn much-needed skills and showed how our work was being recognized.

We all need to work together for common goals. Research shows that when parents, schools and the community work together to support their children, academic performance improves. However, such a vital partnership should not be confined to the ten months of the school year. If we are to significantly improve our children's odds for academic success and reduce the achievement gap, we must build an alliance that lasts throughout the year. When at-risk youth are mentored, schools can expect to see improved student performance, retention and attendance.[106]

As citizens of the United States and of the world, we may not necessarily agree with all components of government, but we are still responsible for the upkeep and improvement of our modern society. One of the greatest challenges of a mentor is to enable an at-risk youth to understand citizenship and how it affects their lives and their futures. Inner-city kids have no real understanding and do not grasp these obligations and responsibilities to the community, nation or world. Mentors can make an impact in the community and even the world when these individuals become tomorrow's leaders. For this reason, I think it is very important to teach at-risk youth about citizenship. They need to understand what it takes to be a good citizen in our community.

Feeling strong and determined to give hope to youths, I instituted an annual youth conference at the Tampa Bay Academy

---

[105] WTMP 96.1FM and 1150AM an Urban radio channel from Tampa, FL.
[106] Deborah Yaffe, "Family: America's Smallest School," ETS Policy Notes, ETS Policy Evaluation & Research Center 19.1: Winter 2011. Report No: PIC-PNV19N1, http://www.ets.org/Media/Research/pdf/PICPN191.pdf. Accessed Apr 2011.

of Hope. One year, the students decided to put on a play, "Shades of Color," for all the attendees from the community. They wanted it to be about hope and how people can work together for a common goal in combating youth issues. They wanted to make a difference in their community.

The characters in the play were a group of teens at the same high school who were dealing with pregnancy, peer pressure and gang violence. The teens were from different backgrounds but learned to work together to rise above the adversities plaguing their lives. Eventually, they came to realize that they could rely on each other for help instead of struggling alone, accept one another and learn that they were more alike than they were different in their struggles.

Subsequent to the play's performance, one of the performers in the play, Asli Omur, a 16 year old sophomore, wrote an article, " 'Shades of Color' helps teens find common ground," that was published by a local newspaper. The article noted what a significant impact the play had on its community. The performers' efforts were not in vain; that night, their authentic portrayals moved the hearts and minds of the entire audience –their tears were real and came from their core beings. They performed what they were themselves experiencing and already knew.

The young writer stated, *"..After the performance, we hugged and laughed. We all felt so good. I thought it was pretty cool that people of different races and religions could get together and become friends. To me, that is truly the definition of "community service."* This is but one example of the willingness of youth to take on their responsibilities, be a part of their community and help to change it for the better.

The play was successful because it instantly made a difference in the lives of the teens watching, who were just like them. The message for the community is that teens just need a little push and some guidance to find the recipe for success and Self-Worth.

Empowered by Self-Worth, it's easy to see it in others. I feel that we are all one in humanity and we have to care about our fellow human beings. I feel that your hurt is mine. Having a strong and positive sense of self is important—without it, we are apathetic and our communities suffer.

When public housing evictions suddenly arose in a poverty-stricken neighborhood in downtown Tampa, it sent shockwaves through the community as it became known that the entire lower income housing project was being torn down. It was to be replaced by a 28-acre redevelopment project through a partnership of The Tampa Housing Authority (THA) and the Banc of America

Community Development Corp. The new plan to improve the entire area through redevelopment would provide a mix of residential, retail and commercial components on 28 acres on the Tampa Housing Authority property up the street from my office in the Tampa community...and that entailed displacing the poor. Surprised, evicted and angry residents, some of whom had lived there for over 30 years, many for most of their lives, came to me asking for my help because they felt their rights were violated and specific parts of state law that regulated the operation of housing authorities were in question.

I became a voice for their concerns and organized a small group of activists in the community to address the residents' issues and concerns of being evicted and moved out unfairly. I became a voice to address the Community Development Corp's $800 million redevelopment project to see if it was unconstitutional. I felt the project was great for the community, but various aspects of the project were in question. My attorneys discovered that the residents were being treated unfairly when records revealed questionable practices. Further, the partnership between the Banc of America and the housing authority posed legal questions, and I brought this before city and county officials to ensure oversight of this project was not lacking and the people were being treated justly. I questioned who was doing the checking to make sure these guys were doing everything they said they would.

I felt compassion and love for these poor residents who were being torn from their homes. Their anger and tears moved me to write the following which I distributed via email to all leaders in the community and to all those who knew of my work with the Tampa Bay Academy of Hope.

Bound by Tears

The tears caused by situations and circumstances in our lives and communities bind us all. If we experience injustice and inequity, we shed tears of pain. Regardless of race, gender or age, tears of pain bind us all. But these tears also have the capacity to bring hope; no longer will our sad tears divide us as citizens of Tampa. We must unite ourselves by the power of change in order to solve our problems and reduce the pain in Hillsborough County that binds us.

Bound together by tears, we can reclaim and unite our families.
Bound together by tears, we can change our economic conditions.
Bound together by tears, we can create jobs that pay livable wages.
Bound together by tears, we can restore our broken schools.
Bound together by tears, we can heal our dysfunctional churches.

Bound together by tears, we can end hunger.
Bound together by tears, we can prevent violence and abuse.
Bound together by tears, we can secure affordable health care for all.

In East, West, South and North Tampa, the passion of our tears binds us all—even when our voices grow weary and powerless. We must battle the tears that connect our pain. Together, we must find faith, hope and determination in our tears of joy and sorrow. We can repair our community by removing the ever-growing self-doubt. Together, we can repair our lives and community by removing the obstacles that tell us there is no hope for today's generation and that our voices are of no effect.

When we face the injustice and inequality together, we have the power to be strong for each other, to heal the wounds that plague our collective minds. Nothing must stand in the way of us calling for community change to deal with the tears that bind us all.

Over the past 15 years, I have earned the respect of the community and the trust of its youth and built a program on the core belief in the value of Human Worth. I have motivated youths to reach their potential and inspired families who, in most cases, have lost hope. I have also emphasized the importance of their need to take responsibility for their community. As youth are given the opportunity to participate in the decisions and future direction of their communities in a meaningful way, they will learn more about both themselves and their community. Rooted in their Human Worth and encouraged by hope, people can have a profound impact on accomplishing real change in their communities. We are fortunate to live in a country where people have the power to unite in a common cause to better their communities...and it's time to get involved.

APPENDIX A

Brief Synopsis of "Who Moved My Cheese?" by Dr. Spencer Johnson, (Putnam Adult, 1998), 94 pgs.

Sniff and Scurry, the little mice, have simple minds and thinking processes while Hem and Haw, the "littlepeople," have complicated ones. Their mission is to "find cheese."

At first, all of them were very hard-working, getting up early and scurrying around the maze looking for cheese, finding bits and pieces here and there until one day they found a room full of cheese. Sitting down to devour the cheese to their hearts' content, Sniff and Scurry hung their running shoes around their necks while Hem and Haw discarded theirs.

After finding the room full of cheese, they went there day after day following the same routine. But then, Hem and Haw started to get lazy, arriving there later and later, thinking the cheese will always be there. One day, the cheese was gone. Sniff and Scurry were already sniffing and scurrying here and there, going round and round in the room wondering where the cheese was. Certain there was no more cheese there, Sniff and Scurry saw what they needed to do—they put on their running shoes and went back into the maze to look for new cheese. They did not hesitate and scurried into action immediately.

Hem and Haw did not follow them, telling them that they were going to wait in the room, hoping the cheese would re-appear the next day. They go to the empty room every day hoping to find new cheese there. They complained and whined to each other, "How can they do this to us?", "Where is our cheese?", "It's not fair...we found the cheese, how can they take it away from us?"

One day, Haw suggested to Hem maybe they should go out and look for new cheese in the maze. Hem thought Haw was crazy believing that it was too dangerous out there, that they wouldn't find any cheese for days, and that there might be traps in the maze. Haw started to waver in his decision. So, they sat there again for days hoping to get new cheese. They became very weak, having not eaten for days. Whenever Haw started thinking about going out into the maze, Hem quickly reminded him of the danger out there.

One day Haw realized that they couldn't possibly get new cheese by staying in the room. After failing to persuade Hem to follow him, he started his journey into the unknown. He found bits and pieces of cheese here and there to sustain him, but no big cheese. Haw hoped that Hem would finally decide to leave and follow his tracks along the maze's wall.

When Sniff and Scurry started their journey in the maze, they diligently looked from one place to another, day after day, until one day they found a new room full of cheese. They were so happy and ate to their hearts' content.

One day while searching, Haw discovered his friends Sniff and Scurry in a room full of many kinds of cheese. They greeted him and continued stuffing themselves. Without wasting any more time, Haw immediately sat down to eat the most delicious cheese he had found in some time. This time, Haw did not discard his running shoes, but hung them around his neck like Sniff and Scurry did. He now realized that he might have to look for new cheese again.

Haw thought about finding Hem and bringing him to enjoy the new cheese but knew that Hem had to make his own decision. He had left enough tracks for Hem to follow if he decided to. Haw had felt frightened of the unknown but now found a new strength in himself. He learned to adapt in time (i.e., before starving) and saw that changing his habits led to something better (i.e., he eventually found the cheese). He also realized that if he had looked carefully while they still had the big cheese, he would have noticed the cheese getting smaller and the taste starting to go bad. Movement in a new direction helps us find "new cheese."

APPENDIX B

LEADERSHIP THROUGH EDUCATION MODEL

The mission of the Tampa Bay Academy of Hope was accomplished through a four-step approach as follows:

1) Outreach recruitment and selection. Students were recruited in partnership with the Hillsborough County School District; eligibility was determined and students were enrolled.

2) Establishment of TBAH Leadership Clubs in the feeder schools. TBAH coaches went to the district schools, rotating every other week to address and monitor student academics, attendance, behavior, Self-Esteem, and leadership skills.

3) Providing support and mentoring programs and services to both youth and their parents. They involved parents in a collaborative way through a Parent Leadership Advocacy Network (PLAN) which put parents in touch with each other, and together they served as a "PTA" for the clubs. They involved youth through a Youth Leadership Council (YLC) which was a youth support group. The YLC gives guidance to the TBAH administration in terms of the academic, social and leadership needs and issues of the youth. The mentoring program was TBAH-based, i.e., all tutoring and other mentor services were structured, organized and controlled by TBAH. Enrichment Activities involved students in year-round programs and activities for jobs and internships and we often referred our students to outside agencies that provided academic or social programs. TBAH encouraged its mentors to support the students in such referred programs.

4) The final component of the Leadership Through Education model involved outcome measurement and evaluation using the 4-D assessment tool (Circle of Hope) and a computer tracking system (System of Hope). The system was designed to assess individual progress, provide informational reports and appraise how program services were meeting their goals. Relevant information (i.e., GPA, disciplinary action, attendance) was collected by TBAH leadership at the beginning of the program period, mid-year and at the end of the program period. Statistical reports were generated quarterly to reflect the participants' development in academic achievement, behavior and attendance. Group reports reflected demographic statistics and process information.

TBAH developed a series of workshops, to specifically address the risk of violent behavior in at-risk children. They were designed to:
- Increase the individual's Self-Confidence through exposure to the concept of Human Worth and through participation in positive community activities
- Provide participants with new tools to handle their violent impulses in a healthy way
- Develop positive connections to adult role models
- Increase school attendance and grade point average
- Reduce the number of incidents participants encounter with illegal, problematic or anti-social behaviors
- Provide classes for parents that provide both education and support

Once a month, students gathered for 2-3 hours to explore four themes used extensively with at-risk youth. These themes were based on the four components of the Circle of Courage: Becoming, Knowing, Belonging and Giving.[107]

Theme One explored the concept of Rising Above Adversity and aligns with the idea of "becoming." Workshops, rap sessions and other activities complemented chapters in the Skills of Hope youth workbooks and asked the question, "Where do I fit in?" Youth were taught how to make positive choices and take control of their own lives. They learned how to plan for their future and make decisions that enhance their autonomy in school and the community. Team-building activities assisted the young people in "becoming" who they are.

Theme Two focused on Building Self-Esteem while aligning with the concept of "knowing." Knowing represents one of the basic building blocks for establishing Self-Worth. It recognizes the importance of doing things well and having pride in your abilities. Self-Worth is enhanced when youth experience control over events in their lives, show a capacity for self-control and have both motivation and abilities to accomplish personal goals. The child who loses his sense of Self-Worth is vulnerable to the negative influences of others. Therefore, TBAH guided youth to identify those tendencies in him/herself. Tools were utilized via a Skills of Hope Youth Workbook, rap sessions and team-building exercises to elevate the youth's Self-Esteem to a healthy, productive level.

Theme Three, Reversing Violent Trends, aligned with "belonging." Many of the youth targeted for this program had witnessed violence from a very young age. Innate survival skills may propel them to a defensive stance, and they may use violence or other inappropriate behaviors as a way to address the challenges in their lives. Using the workbooks and activities, youth were given tools and

---

[107] Larry Brendtro, Martin Brokenleg, & Steve Van Bockern, *Reclaiming Youth at Risk: Our Hope for the Future* (Bloomington, IN: National Educational Service, 1990).

opportunities to "walk the talk" in a positive manner throughout challenging situations.

Finally, **Theme Four** explored the concept of Strengthening Relationships, which aligned with the Circle of Courage concept of "giving." Giving often translates into positive outcomes for both the receiver and the giver. It comes in many forms: time, caring, recognition, material goods, and services. It requires balancing one's own interests with the interests of others and is the foundation of relationship building. TBAH recognized that youth must build positive relationships at school, in the community and especially at home. Participants were engaged in team-building exercises and community activities to reinforce this concept.

An essential component of this program was parental involvement. Therefore, parents were encouraged to attend four workshops specifically tailored to their needs. Discussions and complementary materials aided parents to understand the TBAH philosophy. These workshops enabled the parents to reinforce the lessons their children were learning. The group process also allowed the parents to support one another as they supported their children.

BIBLIOGRAPHY

Adler, Alfred. *What Life Should Mean To You*. London: Unwin Books, 1932.

Atkins, Todd, *Earning Your Worth Through Accomplishment—Human Doing Instead of Human Being*. Baton Rouge Counseling. Jun 8, 2010.
http://batonrougecounseling.net/blog/counseling/earning-worth-accomplishment-human-human/. Accessed Feb 2011.

Ballard, Elizabeth Silance. "Three Letters from Teddy," *Home Life*. March 1976. Citation: "Teddy Stoddard." http://www.truthorfiction.com/rumors/t/teddy.htm. Accessed Oct 2010.

Baumeister, Roy E, Joseph M. Boden and Laura Smart. *Relation of Threatened Egotism to Violence and Aggression: The Dark Side of High Self-Esteem*, The American Psychological Association, Inc., 103.1 (1996): 5-33. Citation: http://www.emotionalcompetency.com/papers/baumeistersmartboden1996%5B1%5D.pdf. Accessed Jun 2010.

Bonhoeffer, Dietrich. *The Cost of Discipleship*. New York: Touchstone, 1995.

Bosak, Susan V. The Legacy project. "What is a Legacy?" http://www.legacyproject.org/about/chair.html. Accessed Jan 2011.

Bradshaw, John. *Healing the Shame That Binds You*. Deerfield Beach, FL: Health Communication, Inc., 2005.

Branden, Nathaniel. *The Psychology of Self-Esteem*. San Francisco, CA: Jossey-Bass, 2001.

Branden, Nathaniel. *Honoring the Self: Self-Esteem and Personal Transformation*. New York: Bantam Books, 1984.

Brendtro, Larry, Martin Brokenleg & Steve Van Bockern. *Reclaiming Youth at Risk: Our Hope for the Future*. Bloomington, IN: National Educational Service, 1990.

Bubniak, Saundra. "Human worth contingent on struggle to survive not cultural criteria." http://www.examiner.com/holistic-health-in-detroit/human-worth-contingent-on-struggle-to-survive-not-cultural-criteria. Accessed Jan 2011.

Buffet, Warren Edward. Quoted in: http://quotationsbook.com/quote/461/. Accessed Aug 2010.

Catalanello, Rebecca. Times Staff Writer. "They Came Looking for Answers." *St Petersburg Times* [FL] Dec 2, 2005. http://www.sptimes.com/2005/12/02/Tampabay/They_came_looking_for.shtml. Accessed Aug 24, 2011.

Center for Disease Control. *Sexual Risk Behavior: HIV, STD and Teen Pregnancy Prevention*. 2009. http://www.cdc.gov/HealthyYouth/sexualbehaviors/. Accessed Aug 24, 2011.

"Cognitive Distortions: Ten Forms of Self-Defeating Thoughts," http://www.psychology-resources.com/library/Cognitive%20Distortions.pdf. Accessed Feb 2011.

Dahklloetter, JoAnn, *Your Performing Edge: The Complete Mind-Body Guide for Excellence in Sports, Health and Life*. San Carlos, CA: Pulgas Ridge Press, 2004.

DeFrank, Daniel K. "The Power to Choose." *New Times*, [Tampa,FL] July/August 2001.

Demuth, S. and S. Brown, "Family Structure, Family Processes and Adolescence Delinquency: The Significance of Parental Absence versus Parental Gender." *Journal of Research in Crime and Delinquency*, 41.1 (Feb 2004): 58-81. http://jrc.sagepub.com/content/41/1/58.short. Accessed Aug 30, 2011.

Dr. Phil, *Self Matters: Defining Your Authentic Self*, http://www.drphil.com/articles/article/73. Accessed Mar 2011.

Evans, James M. *The ABC's of Authentic Hope: Youth Survival Techniques and Life Skills*. Tampa, FL: Eagle Quest Group, 1997.

Evans, James M. *The Autobiography of James M. Evans: Meeting Himself For The Very First Time*. Tampa, FL: Eagle Quest Group, 2005.

Franken, Robert E. *Human Motivation*. 3rd ed. Pacific Grove, CA: Brooks/Cole, 1994. Citation: W. Huitt, *Self and Self-Views*. Educational Psychology Interactive, 2009, Valdosta, GA: Valdosta State Univ., http://www.edpsycinteractive.org/topics/self/self.html. Accessed Nov 2010.

Fromm, Erich. *The Art of Loving*. 1956. Citation: Russell A. Dewey. *Psychology: An Introduction*. http://www.psywww.com/intropsych/ch16_sfl/art_of_loving.html. Accessed Apr 10, 2011.

Goldberg, Steve and Barbara Goldberg. *Finding the Upside: Practical Wisdom for Challenging Times*. www.findingtheupside.org. Citation: Steve Goldberg, *When Net Worth Becomes Self-Worth*. Life As a Human: The Online Magazine for Evolving Minds. Feb 22, 2011. http://lifeasahuman.com/2011/mind-spirit/inspirational/when-net-worth-becomes-self-worth/. Accessed Mar 2011.

Hayes, Gwendolyn. "200 Youth To Benefit From Youth Leadership Conference." *The Florida Sentinel* 13 Sept 2002.

Holton, Iris B. "At-Risk Program Draws Attention of FAMU Research Program." *The Florida Sentinel-Bulletin* 23 Apr 2010.

Holton, Iris B. "Skills of Hope Youth Leadership Conference 2004." *The Florida Sentinel-Bulletin* 15 Aug 2004.

Holton, Iris B. "Study Cites Organization For Work With Juveniles." *The Florida Sentinel-Bulletin* 26 Aug 2003.

Hooper, Ernest. "With Soft Words, Turning Kids—From Trouble." *St Petersburg Times* [FL] 10 Sept 2004.

Huitt, W. *Self and self-views*. *Educational Psychology Interactive*. 2009. Valdosta, GA: Valdosta State Univ., , http://www.edpsycinteractive.org/topics/self/self.html. Accessed Nov 2010.

Johnson, Spencer. *Who Moved My Cheese? An Amazing Way To Deal With Change In Your Work And In Your Life*. New York: Putnam Adult, 1998.

Kennedy, M. "Self-Determination and Trust: My Experiences and Thoughts," In D.J. Sands & M. Wehmeyer, eds. *Self-Determination Across the Life Span: Independence and choice for people with disabilities*. Baltimore, MD: Paul H. Brookes, 1996.

Klibert, Jeffrey J., Jennifer Langhinrichsen-Rohling, & Motoko Saito. "Adaptive and Maladaptive Aspects of Self-Oriented versus Socially Prescribed Perfectionism," *Journal of College Student Development* 46:2, (March/April 2005): 141-156.

Lux, Heidi. "James Evans and Tampa Bay Academy of Hope Holds Faces of Hope Black Tie Gala and Fundraiser 2009" *Tampa Bay Informer-Clearwater*. 14 Jul 2009.

Maslow, Abraham H. *Motivation and Personality*. New York: Harper and Row, 1954. Citation: Tom G. Stevens, *You Can Choose To Be Happy*. Chap 5, Part 3. Self-Acceptance, The Keys to Eliminating Guilt and Anger. http://www.csulb.edu/~tstevens/h53accep.htm. Accessed Mar 2011.

Maslow, Abraham H. *A Theory of Human Motivation*. Psychological Review, 50 (1943): 381. Citation: Christoper D. Green. *The Esteem Needs*. Classics in the History of Psychology. http://psychclassics.yorku.ca/Maslow/motivation.htm. Accessed Aug 2011.

Mercer, Johnny. "Accentuate The Positive." Capital-EMI record label. 1945.

The National Campaign to Prevent Teen and Unplanned Pregnancy. *Campaign Update Summer 2001*. p 9. Citation: http://www.thenationalcampaign.org/about-us/PDF/Summer2001update.pdf. Accessed Sept 12, 2011.

Nichols, Ralph G. "The Struggle To Be Human." University of Minnesota ILA Convention: Atlanta, Georgia, Feb 17, 1980. http://casts.webvalence.com/sites/ListeningLeader/Broadcast.D20051109.html. Accessed Oct 2010.

Nova, Elisa. "Elephant Aggression on Humans and Rhinos." Opinion/Editorial, Nov 9, 2006. http://www.associatedcontent.com/article/80375/elephant_aggression_on_humans_and_rhinos.html?cat=9. Accessed Nov 2010.

"NRS Statistics on Runaways." In "National Runaway Switchboard." 2011. http://www.1800runaway.org/learn/research/third_party/. Accessed Aug 24, 2011.

"The NSDUH Report: Depression and the Initiation of Alcohol and Other Drug Use among Youths Aged 12 to 17." Substance Abuse & Mental Health Services Administration, U.S. Department of Health & Human Services. 2005. http://www.oas.samhsa.gov/2k7/newUserDepression/newUserDepression.cfm. Accessed Aug 24, 2011.

"The NSDUH Report: Driving Under the Influence (DUI) Among Young Persons." Substance Abuse & Mental Health Services Administration, U.S. Department of Health & Human Services. (2003). http://www.oas.samhsa.gov/DWI.htm. Accessed Aug 24, 2011.

Office of the Surgeon General. "Youth Violence: A Report of the Surgeon General." 2000. http://www.surgeongeneral.gov/library/youthviolence. Accessed Jan 28, 2010.

Pant Hoot quarterly newsletter, Issue 1, Winter 2006. www.janegoodall.org.

Robbins, Anthony. Awaken the Giant Within. New York: Free Press, 1992.

Roberts, Mark D. "Dan Rather, Meet Teddy Stallard," Oct 11, 2004. http://www.christianitytoday.com/le/currenttrendscolumns/leadershipweekly/cln41011.html. Accessed Oct 2010.

Roy, Kenneth G. "The Systemic Conditions Leading To Violent Human Behavior." Journal of Applied Behavioral Science, 36, Dec 2000: 389-407. http://www.jab.sagepub.com/content/36/4/389.full.pdf. Accessed Jan 2011.

"Sarcasm is the Key to Our Bonding," Parade magazine, 17 Jan 2010, p 5.

Stevens, Tom G. You Can Choose To Be Happy, 2010, Chap 5, Part 3. Self-Acceptance, http://www.csulb.edu/~tstevens/h53accep.htm. Accessed Mar 2011.

"Charles R. Swindoll quotes. " Thinkexist.com. http://thinkexist.com/quotes/charles_r._swindoll/. Accessed Nov 2010.

Tyler, R. W. "The Development Of Instruments For Assessing Educational Progress." In Proceedings of the 1965 invitational conference on testing problems. Princeton, NJ: Educational Testing Service, 1966, 95-105.

Vansickle, Abbie. "One citizen's quest for justice." St Petersburg Times [FL], 17 Jun 2007. http://www.sptimes.com/2007/06/17/Hillsborough/One_citizen_s_quest_f.shtml. Accessed Oct 2010.

Vujicic, Nick. Life Without Limbs. http://press.lifewithoutlimbs.org/. Accessed Aug 23, 2011.

What's Love Got to do With It? Dir. Brian Gibson. Perf. Angela Bassett, Laurence Fishburne. Touchstone Production Co., 1993.

Yaffe, Deborah. "The Family: America's Smallest School." ETS Policy Notes. ETS Policy Evaluation & Research Center. 19. 1: Winter 2011. Report No: PIC-PNV19N1. http://www.ets.org/Media/Research/pdf/PICPN191.pdf. Accessed Apr 2011.

Ziv, Talia, Life Satisfaction & Quality of Life Coaching. http://www.drtaliaziv.com/6.html. Accessed Mar 2011.

Ziv, Talia, Relational Resilience Coaching. http://www.drtaliaziv.com/7.html. Accessed Mar 2011.

FURTHER READING

Blanchard, Ken, Thad Lacinak, Chuck Tompkins & Jim Ballard. *Whale Done: The Power of Positive Relationships*. New York: The Free Press, 2002.

Booher, Dianna. *Communicate with Confidence!* New York: McGraw-Hill, Inc., 1994.

Covey, Stephen R. *The 7 Habits of Highly Effective People*. New York: Free Press, 2004.

Dungy, Tony. *Quiet Strength*. Carol Stream, IL:Tyndale House Publishers, Inc., 2007.

Evans, James M. *The ABC's of Authentic Hope: Youth Survival Techniques and Life Skills*. Tampa, FL: Eagle Quest Group, 1997.

Greenleaf Center, *Insights on Leadership*. New York: John Wiley and Sons, Inc., 1998.

Henry, D. (2000). "Peer groups, families and school failure among urban children: Elements of risk and successful interventions." *Preventing School Failure, 44*, 97-104.

Hill, Napoleon & W. Clement Stone. *Success, Through A Positive Mental* Attitude. Upper Saddle River, NJ: Prentice-Hall, Inc., 1990.

Green, Bob & Oprah Winfrey. *Make the Connection*. New York: Hyperion, 1996.

McClelland, David C. *Human Motivation*. New York: Cambridge University Press, 1987.

Stanley, Charley. *The Reason For My Hope*. Nashville, TN: Thomas Nelson, Inc., 1997.

Swindoll, Charles R. *Great Attitudes! 10 Choices for Success in Life*. Nashville, TN: Thomas Nelson Inc., 2006.

Wolin, Steven J. & Sybil Wolin, *The Resilient Self*. New York: Vallard Books, 1994.

ABOUT THE AUTHOR

James M. Evans has more than two decades of experience working with companies and organizations, community boards, churches, individuals, youth, and parents during which time he has served as mentor, life-coach, counselor, community organizer, church elder, founder of a non-profit, and consultant. He has also been well-received as a passionate and inspiring motivational speaker, well-known throughout the Tampa Bay community and counties in the state of Florida, and has received numerous awards and certificates for his community work.

Born in 1963 in rural Alabama, the 17th of 21 children, to a single mother who had only a 3rd grade education, he experienced a life of poverty throughout his childhood. He lost interest in school at a very young age, which led to him being labeled "educationally mentally retarded." However, when he entered middle school, he met a coach who provided the necessary guidance needed to improve his academics and social skill and, more significantly, his athletic ability on the football field. Mr. Evans became one of the top running backs for Blount High School in Prichard, Alabama, and earned a full football scholarship to Southern University in Baton Rouge, Louisiana. Despite all of the struggles he experienced early in life, in 1987 he was privileged to experience what most inner-city kids could only dream of—he was drafted into the NFL by the Kansas City Chiefs and later by the Tampa Bay Buccaneers. While living his dream of being a professional football player, he discovered that he also possessed the gift of public speaking and could use it to make a difference in the lives of others. He soon realized that his true calling was not on the football field—his passion was to be of service to others and make a difference in the world. In 1996, he founded the Tampa Bay Academy of Hope (TBAH), a leading non-profit organization in Tampa, Florida. While leading TBAH, he raised over $10 million dollars for youth projects in his community to benefit inner-city children and impacted and improved the lives of over 100,000 TBAH participants through an exemplary educational and mentoring program.

Mr. Evans' life is a true testimony of the Power of Human Worth! His difficult life experiences enabled him to discover the key to overcoming life's challenges—understanding the Power of Human Worth. He continues to be a much sought-after motivational speaker on the *Fundamentals of the Power of Human Worth*; his presentation style is highly rated by all audiences. His desire to reach a larger audience and serve others is what motivated him to write this book, *The Power of Human Worth*. His motto is: *"The greatest essential in life is service to others, so keep serving others."*

CPSIA information can be obtained at www.ICGtesting.com
Printed in the USA
LVOW08s1847280914

406254LV00026B/1318/P